# AI REVOLUTION:

## Navigating the Future of Artificial Intelligence and Technology Trends

### William Palmer

# CONTENTS

Title Page
Prologue
Chapter 1: Introduction to Artificial Intelligence and Technology Trends ... 1
Chapter 2: Historical Development of Artificial Intelligence ... 5
Chapter 3: Core Concepts of Artificial Intelligence ... 10
Chapter 4: Current Trends in Artificial Intelligence ... 16
Chapter 5: AI and the Internet of Things (IoT) ... 23
Chapter 6: Big Data and AI ... 30
Chapter 7: AI in Business and Industry ... 37
Chapter 8: AI and Automation ... 44
Chapter 9: Ethics and AI ... 51
Chapter 10: Future Trends in AI ... 57
Chapter 11: AI Tools and Platforms ... 64
Chapter 12: Case Studies ... 71
Chapter 13: The Future of Work with AI ... 78
Chapter 14: AI Research and Development ... 85
Chapter 15: Building an AI Strategy ... 92
Chapter 16: AI in Everyday Life ... 99
Chapter 17: AI and Cybersecurity ... 107
Chapter 18: Interdisciplinary Approaches to AI ... 114

| | |
|---|---|
| Chapter 19: Educational Resources for AI | 122 |
| Chapter 20: Conclusion | 129 |
| Citation List | 135 |
| Epilogue | 139 |

# PROLOGUE

In the early 21st century, the world stood on the brink of a technological revolution unlike any other. Artificial Intelligence (AI), once confined to the realms of science fiction and academic research, began to emerge as a transformative force, poised to reshape industries, redefine the workforce, and revolutionize everyday life. As we navigate through this era of rapid advancements, understanding the intricacies of AI and its vast potential becomes imperative.

"AI Revolution: Navigating the Future of Artificial Intelligence and Technology Trends" is born out of a desire to demystify AI and provide a comprehensive guide to this dynamic and ever-evolving field. This book aims to equip readers with the knowledge and insights necessary to grasp the profound impact of AI, explore its diverse applications, and address the ethical considerations that accompany its development and deployment.

Our journey begins with an exploration of the historical milestones that have shaped AI, tracing its evolution from early theoretical concepts to modern-day advancements. As we delve into the core concepts of AI, including machine learning, deep learning, and natural language processing, we uncover the foundational technologies that drive AI's capabilities.

Throughout this book, we will venture into various industries, showcasing how AI is transforming healthcare, finance, retail, manufacturing, and transportation. Real-world case studies highlight the successes and challenges faced by organizations implementing AI, providing valuable lessons and insights.

Beyond industrial applications, AI intersects with creativity, scientific research, and public safety, demonstrating its versatility and potential to address complex global challenges. We will explore these interdisciplinary applications, revealing how AI fosters innovation and enhances human ingenuity.

However, the rise of AI also brings forth significant ethical considerations. Issues of privacy, bias, fairness, and accountability are critical to ensuring that AI technologies benefit society as a whole. We will discuss these ethical challenges and propose strategies for developing and deploying AI responsibly.

As we look to the future, emerging trends such as quantum computing, explainable AI, and federated learning promise to push the boundaries of what AI can achieve. Integration with other cutting-edge technologies like the Internet of Things (IoT) and blockchain will further expand AI's capabilities and applications.

"AI Revolution" is not just a book about technology; it is a guide for navigating the complexities of AI in a world that is increasingly influenced by intelligent systems. Whether you are a professional seeking to implement AI in your business, a student aspiring to enter the field, or simply an enthusiast eager to learn more, this book is designed to provide you with the tools and knowledge to thrive in the AI-driven future.

Join us on this journey as we explore the revolutionary potential of AI, uncover its transformative impact across various domains, and chart a course towards a future where AI enhances and enriches human life. Welcome to the AI revolution.

# CHAPTER 1: INTRODUCTION TO ARTIFICIAL INTELLIGENCE AND TECHNOLOGY TRENDS

**What is Artificial Intelligence?**

Artificial Intelligence (AI) refers to the simulation of human intelligence in machines that are programmed to think, learn, and adapt. These systems use algorithms and data to make decisions, solve problems, and perform tasks that typically require human intelligence. AI can range from simple systems that perform specific tasks to more complex systems capable of learning and evolving over time.

**Significance of AI in Modern Technology**

Artificial Intelligence is revolutionizing the way we live and work. Its integration into modern technology is transforming industries, enhancing productivity, and fostering innovation. Here are several ways AI is significant in today's world:

1. **Automation and Efficiency**: AI automates repetitive tasks, freeing up human resources for more complex and creative work. This increases efficiency and reduces the likelihood of errors.

2. **Data Analysis and Insights**: AI can analyze vast amounts of data at unprecedented speeds, uncovering patterns and insights that humans might miss. This capability is essential in fields such as finance, healthcare, and marketing.
3. **Personalization**: AI algorithms enable personalized experiences in e-commerce, entertainment, and digital marketing by analyzing user behavior and preferences.
4. **Enhanced User Experience**: AI-powered chatbots and virtual assistants provide instant customer service, improving user satisfaction and engagement.
5. **Innovation and Problem Solving**: AI fosters innovation by providing tools for solving complex problems, from drug discovery in pharmaceuticals to climate modeling in environmental science.

**The Impact of AI on Various Industries**

AI's transformative power extends across multiple sectors, driving significant changes and advancements. Here are a few examples:

1. **Healthcare**

    - **Diagnostics and Treatment**: AI algorithms analyze medical images and patient data to assist in diagnosing diseases and recommending treatments. For instance, AI is used to detect early signs of cancer in radiology scans.
    - **Drug Discovery**: AI accelerates the drug discovery process by predicting how different compounds will interact with biological targets, significantly reducing the time and cost involved.

2. **Finance**

    - **Fraud Detection**: AI systems analyze transaction patterns to detect fraudulent activities in real-time, providing enhanced security for financial institutions

and their customers.
- **Algorithmic Trading**: AI-powered trading systems execute trades at high speeds based on complex algorithms, optimizing investment strategies and increasing market efficiency.

3. **Retail and E-commerce**
   - **Personalized Recommendations**: AI analyzes customer behavior to provide personalized product recommendations, enhancing the shopping experience and increasing sales.
   - **Inventory Management**: AI forecasts demand and optimizes inventory levels, reducing costs and ensuring product availability.

4. **Manufacturing**
   - **Predictive Maintenance**: AI monitors equipment performance and predicts failures before they occur, minimizing downtime and maintenance costs.
   - **Quality Control**: AI systems inspect products for defects, ensuring high-quality standards and reducing waste.

5. **Transportation**
   - **Autonomous Vehicles**: AI powers self-driving cars, enhancing safety and efficiency in transportation.
   - **Traffic Management**: AI analyzes traffic patterns to optimize traffic flow, reducing congestion and travel times.

6. **Entertainment**
   - **Content Creation**: AI is used to create music, art, and literature, pushing the boundaries of creativity.
   - **Personalized Streaming**: AI algorithms recommend

movies, shows, and music based on user preferences, enhancing the entertainment experience.

## The Importance of Staying Updated with AI Trends

Staying updated with AI trends is crucial for several reasons:

1. **Competitive Advantage**: Businesses that leverage the latest AI technologies gain a competitive edge by improving efficiency, enhancing customer experiences, and driving innovation.
2. **Adaptation and Resilience**: Understanding AI trends helps organizations adapt to technological changes and remain resilient in a rapidly evolving landscape.
3. **Informed Decision-Making**: Knowledge of AI trends enables informed decision-making, ensuring investments in technology align with current and future needs.
4. **Skill Development**: For professionals, staying updated with AI trends is essential for career growth. It ensures they possess the skills needed in an AI-driven job market.
5. **Ethical Considerations**: Awareness of AI developments helps stakeholders address ethical issues, such as bias, privacy, and the impact of automation on jobs, fostering responsible AI use.

## Conclusion

In this chapter, we've introduced the fundamental concepts of Artificial Intelligence and highlighted its significance in modern technology. We've explored the impact of AI across various industries and emphasized the importance of staying updated with AI trends. As we delve deeper into this ebook, we'll uncover the historical development of AI, core concepts, current and future trends, ethical considerations, and practical applications. By understanding the evolving landscape of AI, readers can better appreciate its transformative potential and harness its power to drive innovation and growth in their respective fields.

# CHAPTER 2: HISTORICAL DEVELOPMENT OF ARTIFICIAL INTELLIGENCE

**Introduction**

The journey of Artificial Intelligence (AI) from a theoretical concept to a transformative force in modern technology spans several decades. This chapter explores the key historical milestones that have shaped the field of AI, highlighting significant developments and breakthroughs from its early research days to contemporary advancements.

**Early Foundations of AI (1940s-1950s)**

1. **Alan Turing and the Turing Test**
   - **Turing's Vision**: Alan Turing, often considered the father of AI, laid the groundwork for the field with his 1950 paper "Computing Machinery and Intelligence." He proposed the idea that machines could simulate any human intelligence process.
   - **The Turing Test**: Turing introduced the Turing Test, a criterion for determining whether a machine exhibits human-like intelligence. A machine passes the test if it

can engage in a conversation indistinguishable from a human.

2. **Early Computers and AI Concepts**
   - **ENIAC and UNIVAC**: The development of early computers like ENIAC (1945) and UNIVAC (1951) provided the necessary hardware for AI research.
   - **Cybernetics**: Norbert Wiener's work on cybernetics in the 1940s explored control and communication in animals and machines, influencing early AI thinking.

## The Birth of AI (1956-1970s)

3. **Dartmouth Conference (1956)**
   - **AI as a Field**: The Dartmouth Conference, organized by John McCarthy, Marvin Minsky, Nathaniel Rochester, and Claude Shannon, is considered the birth of AI as a field. They coined the term "Artificial Intelligence" and discussed the potential of machines to simulate human intelligence.

4. **Early AI Programs**
   - **Logic Theorist**: Developed by Allen Newell and Herbert A. Simon in 1955, the Logic Theorist was one of the first AI programs, designed to mimic human problem-solving skills.
   - **General Problem Solver (GPS)**: Also created by Newell and Simon, GPS (1957) aimed to solve a wide range of problems using a general-purpose algorithm.

5. **Natural Language Processing**
   - **ELIZA**: In 1966, Joseph Weizenbaum created ELIZA, an early natural language processing program that could simulate a conversation with a human by using pattern matching techniques.

## The AI Winter and Renewed Interest (1970s-1990s)

6. **The First AI Winter**

- **Funding Cuts and Challenges**: The 1970s saw reduced funding and interest in AI research due to unmet expectations and technological limitations, leading to the first "AI Winter."

7. **Expert Systems**
   - **MYCIN**: Developed in the 1970s, MYCIN was an expert system for diagnosing bacterial infections and recommending treatments. It demonstrated the potential of AI in specialized domains.
   - **R1/XCON**: Created by Digital Equipment Corporation in the 1980s, R1 (later known as XCON) was an expert system used to configure computer systems. It became one of the first successful commercial AI applications.

8. **Neural Networks and Backpropagation**
   - **Perceptrons and Early Neural Networks**: In the 1960s, Frank Rosenblatt developed the Perceptron, an early neural network model. However, its limitations were highlighted by Marvin Minsky and Seymour Papert in their 1969 book "Perceptrons."
   - **Backpropagation Algorithm**: In the 1980s, the development of the backpropagation algorithm by Geoffrey Hinton, David Rumelhart, and Ronald Williams revitalized interest in neural networks by enabling the training of multi-layer networks.

## The Rise of Machine Learning (1990s-2010s)

9. **Reinforcement Learning**
   - **Q-Learning**: In 1989, Christopher Watkins introduced Q-Learning, a model-free reinforcement learning algorithm that became foundational in the field.

10. **Support Vector Machines (SVM)**
    - **Vladimir Vapnik and Alexey Chervonenkis**: In the 1990s, they developed the SVM algorithm, which

became a powerful tool for classification and regression tasks in machine learning.
11. **Big Data and AI**
    - **Data-Driven Approaches**: The late 1990s and early 2000s saw the rise of big data, providing the vast amounts of data needed to train AI models effectively.
12. **Deep Learning Breakthroughs**
    - **ImageNet and AlexNet**: In 2012, Geoffrey Hinton, Alex Krizhevsky, and Ilya Sutskever's AlexNet won the ImageNet competition, significantly advancing the field of computer vision and demonstrating the power of deep learning.

**Modern-Day AI Advancements (2010s-Present)**

13. **AI in Everyday Applications**
    - **Siri, Alexa, and Google Assistant**: The introduction of virtual assistants like Apple's Siri (2011), Amazon's Alexa (2014), and Google Assistant (2016) brought AI into everyday consumer use.
14. **AlphaGo and Reinforcement Learning**
    - **DeepMind's AlphaGo**: In 2016, DeepMind's AlphaGo defeated world champion Go player Lee Sedol, showcasing the potential of reinforcement learning and neural networks in complex strategic games.
15. **Generative Adversarial Networks (GANs)**
    - **Ian Goodfellow**: In 2014, Ian Goodfellow introduced GANs, a class of AI algorithms used to generate realistic data, such as images and videos, through a competitive process between two neural networks.
16. **Natural Language Processing (NLP)**
    - **Transformers and BERT**: The introduction of the transformer architecture in 2017 and models like BERT (2018) revolutionized NLP, enabling more accurate and

context-aware language understanding.
17. **AI in Healthcare**
    - **AI for Disease Diagnosis**: AI models have been developed for diagnosing diseases from medical images, predicting patient outcomes, and personalizing treatment plans, demonstrating AI's transformative potential in healthcare.
18. **Ethical AI and Fairness**
    - **AI Ethics Initiatives**: The 2010s and 2020s have seen growing awareness of the ethical implications of AI, with initiatives focused on ensuring fairness, transparency, and accountability in AI systems.

**Conclusion**

The historical development of Artificial Intelligence is marked by periods of rapid progress, challenges, and renewed interest. From the foundational theories proposed by pioneers like Alan Turing to the cutting-edge advancements in deep learning and natural language processing, AI has evolved significantly over the decades. Understanding this history provides valuable context for appreciating the current state of AI and anticipating future trends and innovations.

# CHAPTER 3: CORE CONCEPTS OF ARTIFICIAL INTELLIGENCE

**Introduction**

Artificial Intelligence (AI) encompasses a broad range of technologies and methodologies designed to mimic human intelligence and perform tasks that typically require human cognitive abilities. This chapter delves into the fundamental concepts of AI, including machine learning, deep learning, neural networks, natural language processing, and computer vision. We will explore how each technology works and its various applications across different industries.

**Machine Learning**

1. **Definition and Overview**
   - Machine learning is a subset of AI that involves the use of algorithms and statistical models to enable computers to improve their performance on tasks through experience.
   - Unlike traditional programming, where explicit instructions are provided, machine learning algorithms learn patterns from data and make decisions based on this learned knowledge.

2. **Types of Machine Learning**
   - **Supervised Learning**: Algorithms are trained on labeled data, where the input-output pairs are known. Applications include image classification, spam detection, and predictive modeling.
   - **Unsupervised Learning**: Algorithms are used on unlabeled data to identify hidden patterns or intrinsic structures. Common techniques include clustering (e.g., customer segmentation) and dimensionality reduction (e.g., Principal Component Analysis).
   - **Reinforcement Learning**: Algorithms learn by interacting with an environment and receiving feedback in the form of rewards or penalties. Applications include game playing (e.g., AlphaGo) and robotic control.

3. **Key Algorithms**
   - **Linear Regression**: Used for predicting a continuous variable based on the linear relationship between the input and output.
   - **Decision Trees**: Tree-like models used for classification and regression tasks, breaking down decisions into a series of simple rules.
   - **Support Vector Machines (SVM)**: Classification algorithm that finds the optimal boundary between different classes in the feature space.
   - **K-Means Clustering**: An unsupervised learning algorithm that partitions data into K clusters based on feature similarity.

## Deep Learning

1. **Definition and Overview**
   - Deep learning is a subset of machine learning that involves neural networks with many layers (deep neural networks). It is particularly effective for large-scale data

and complex tasks.
- Deep learning models automatically learn feature representations from raw data, making them highly effective for tasks like image and speech recognition.

2. **Neural Networks**
    - **Artificial Neural Networks (ANNs):** Modeled after the human brain, consisting of interconnected neurons (nodes) organized in layers. Each neuron processes input and passes the output to the next layer.
    - **Layers in ANNs:**
        - **Input Layer:** Receives the input data.
        - **Hidden Layers:** Perform intermediate processing, with each layer extracting higher-level features.
        - **Output Layer:** Produces the final prediction or classification.

3. **Convolutional Neural Networks (CNNs)**
    - Specialized neural networks for processing grid-like data such as images. They use convolutional layers to detect local patterns (e.g., edges, textures).
    - Applications include image and video recognition, object detection, and medical image analysis.

4. **Recurrent Neural Networks (RNNs)**
    - Designed for sequential data, where the output at one time step depends on the previous time steps. RNNs have connections that form directed cycles, allowing them to maintain memory.
    - Applications include language modeling, machine translation, and time series prediction.

5. **Generative Adversarial Networks (GANs)**
    - Comprise two neural networks, a generator and a discriminator, that compete with each other. The generator creates fake data, while the discriminator tries to distinguish between real and fake data.
    - Applications include image generation, video synthesis,

and data augmentation.

**Natural Language Processing (NLP)**

1. **Definition and Overview**
    - NLP is a field of AI focused on the interaction between computers and human (natural) languages. It enables machines to understand, interpret, and generate human language.
2. **Key Techniques and Models**
    - **Tokenization**: Splitting text into individual words or phrases (tokens).
    - **Part-of-Speech Tagging**: Identifying the grammatical parts of speech in a text (nouns, verbs, adjectives, etc.).
    - **Named Entity Recognition (NER)**: Identifying entities such as names, dates, and locations in text.
    - **Sentiment Analysis**: Determining the sentiment or emotion expressed in a text (positive, negative, neutral).
3. **Advanced NLP Models**
    - **Transformers**: Deep learning models that use attention mechanisms to process entire sentences simultaneously. The Transformer architecture has become the foundation for many state-of-the-art NLP models.
    - **BERT (Bidirectional Encoder Representations from Transformers)**: A transformer-based model that pre-trains deep bidirectional representations, allowing it to understand context from both directions in a sentence.
    - **GPT (Generative Pre-trained Transformer)**: A transformer-based model designed for generating human-like text, widely used for text completion, summarization, and dialogue generation.
4. **Applications**
    - **Machine Translation**: Translating text from one language to another (e.g., Google Translate).

- **Chatbots and Virtual Assistants**: Conversational agents that provide customer support and personal assistance (e.g., Siri, Alexa).
- **Text Summarization**: Automatically generating concise summaries of long documents.
- **Speech Recognition and Synthesis**: Converting spoken language to text and vice versa.

## Computer Vision

1. **Definition and Overview**
   - Computer vision is a field of AI that enables machines to interpret and understand visual information from the world, such as images and videos.

2. **Key Techniques**
   - **Image Classification**: Assigning a label to an entire image (e.g., identifying objects in a photo).
   - **Object Detection**: Identifying and locating multiple objects within an image (e.g., detecting cars and pedestrians in a street scene).
   - **Image Segmentation**: Dividing an image into segments to identify different objects or regions (e.g., segmenting medical images to identify tumors).

3. **Convolutional Neural Networks (CNNs)**
   - CNNs are the backbone of many computer vision applications. They use convolutional layers to automatically learn spatial hierarchies of features from input images.

4. **Applications**
   - **Facial Recognition**: Identifying or verifying individuals based on their facial features.
   - **Autonomous Vehicles**: Enabling self-driving cars to recognize and respond to their environment.
   - **Medical Imaging**: Analyzing medical images to assist in diagnosis and treatment planning.

- **Augmented Reality (AR):** Overlaying digital information on the real world to enhance user experience.

**Conclusion**

This chapter has explored the core concepts of Artificial Intelligence, including machine learning, deep learning, neural networks, natural language processing, and computer vision. Each technology plays a crucial role in the advancement of AI and has numerous applications across different industries. Understanding these fundamental concepts is essential for appreciating the transformative potential of AI and its impact on various aspects of our lives.

# CHAPTER 4: CURRENT TRENDS IN ARTIFICIAL INTELLIGENCE

**Introduction**

Artificial Intelligence (AI) is rapidly evolving and transforming various industries by enhancing efficiency, accuracy, and innovation. This chapter discusses the current trends in AI and explores how it is revolutionizing healthcare, finance, education, transportation, and entertainment. By examining specific implementations and their benefits, we can appreciate the profound impact AI has on these sectors.

**AI in Healthcare**

1. **Diagnostics and Predictive Analytics**

    - **AI in Medical Imaging**: AI algorithms analyze medical images (X-rays, MRIs, CT scans) to detect diseases such as cancer, heart disease, and neurological disorders with high accuracy. For example, Google's DeepMind developed an AI system that can diagnose eye diseases as accurately as world-leading doctors.

    - **Predictive Analytics**: AI models predict patient outcomes and disease progression, allowing for early intervention and personalized treatment plans. IBM Watson Health's AI platform, for example, helps oncologists develop personalized cancer treatment plans by analyzing vast amounts of medical data.

2. **Telemedicine and Virtual Health Assistants**

    ◦ **Telemedicine Platforms**: AI-powered telemedicine platforms provide remote consultations, diagnostics, and treatment recommendations, improving access to healthcare, especially in underserved areas. Companies like Teladoc use AI to enhance telehealth services.

    ◦ **Virtual Health Assistants**: AI-driven virtual assistants like Sensely's Molly offer 24/7 patient support, answering health-related questions, providing medication reminders, and monitoring chronic conditions.

3. **Drug Discovery and Development**

    ◦ **AI in Drug Discovery**: AI accelerates drug discovery by predicting how different compounds will interact with biological targets, significantly reducing the time and cost involved. Insilico Medicine uses AI to identify new drug candidates and predict their efficacy.

    ◦ **Clinical Trials Optimization**: AI optimizes clinical trial design, patient recruitment, and data analysis, increasing the efficiency and success rate of trials. Companies like BenevolentAI leverage AI to enhance clinical research.

**AI in Finance**

1. **Fraud Detection and Prevention**

    ◦ **AI for Fraud Detection**: AI algorithms analyze transaction patterns to detect and prevent fraudulent activities in real-time. PayPal uses machine learning models to identify potentially fraudulent transactions and protect users from financial fraud.

    ◦ **Risk Management**: AI assesses credit risk by analyzing

a wide range of data points, enabling more accurate lending decisions. Zest AI uses AI to provide fair and transparent credit decisions, improving access to credit.

2. **Algorithmic Trading and Investment Management**

    ○ **Algorithmic Trading**: AI-powered trading systems execute trades at high speeds based on complex algorithms, optimizing investment strategies and increasing market efficiency. Firms like Renaissance Technologies use AI for quantitative trading.

    ○ **Robo-Advisors**: AI-driven robo-advisors provide personalized investment advice and portfolio management, democratizing access to financial planning services. Betterment and Wealthfront are examples of companies offering AI-based investment solutions.

3. **Customer Service and Personal Finance Management**

    ○ **AI in Customer Service**: AI chatbots and virtual assistants handle customer inquiries, provide financial advice, and perform transactions, enhancing customer experience. Bank of America's Erica is an AI-driven virtual assistant that helps customers with various banking tasks.

    ○ **Personal Finance Management**: AI applications like Mint and YNAB analyze spending patterns, create budgets, and offer personalized financial advice, helping users manage their finances effectively.

## AI in Education

1. **Personalized Learning and Adaptive Technologies**

    ○ **AI in Personalized Learning**: AI systems analyze students' learning styles, strengths, and weaknesses to provide customized learning experiences. Platforms

like Khan Academy use AI to tailor educational content to individual needs.
- **Adaptive Learning Technologies**: AI-powered adaptive learning platforms adjust the difficulty of exercises based on student performance, ensuring optimal learning progression. Smart Sparrow offers adaptive learning tools for educators to create personalized learning experiences.

2. **AI Tutors and Virtual Learning Assistants**

- **AI Tutors**: AI-driven tutoring systems provide real-time assistance and feedback to students, improving learning outcomes. Carnegie Learning's MATHia is an AI-based tutor that helps students with math concepts.
- **Virtual Learning Assistants**: AI-powered virtual assistants support teachers and students by answering questions, providing additional resources, and facilitating administrative tasks. IBM Watson Education Assistant is an example of an AI assistant used in educational settings.

3. **Content Creation and Grading**

- **AI in Content Creation**: AI tools generate educational content, such as quizzes, exercises, and lesson plans, saving teachers time and effort. Content technologies like Knewton create adaptive learning materials based on AI.
- **Automated Grading**: AI systems grade assignments and exams, providing instant feedback and allowing educators to focus on more complex teaching tasks. Turnitin's AI-driven grading tool assesses student writing for originality and quality.

## AI in Transportation

1. **Autonomous Vehicles and Self-Driving Cars**

- **Self-Driving Technology**: AI powers autonomous vehicles by enabling them to perceive their environment, make decisions, and navigate safely. Companies like Waymo and Tesla are at the forefront of developing self-driving cars.
- **Enhanced Safety and Efficiency**: AI in autonomous vehicles reduces human error, improves road safety, and optimizes traffic flow. AI-based systems like Mobileye provide advanced driver-assistance features that enhance vehicle safety.

2. **Traffic Management and Optimization**

   - **AI in Traffic Management**: AI systems analyze traffic data to optimize traffic signals, reduce congestion, and improve traffic flow. For instance, AI-powered traffic management systems in cities like Pittsburgh adjust signal timings based on real-time traffic conditions.
   - **Predictive Maintenance**: AI monitors the health of transportation infrastructure and vehicles, predicting maintenance needs and preventing breakdowns. Siemens uses AI to predict and address maintenance issues in public transportation systems.

3. **Smart Logistics and Supply Chain Management**

   - **AI in Logistics**: AI optimizes logistics and supply chain operations by predicting demand, optimizing routes, and managing inventory. Companies like DHL use AI to enhance their logistics processes and improve efficiency.
   - **Automated Warehousing**: AI-driven robots and systems manage warehousing operations, increasing accuracy and reducing costs. Amazon's fulfillment centers employ AI-powered robots for sorting and managing inventory.

## AI in Entertainment

1. **Content Creation and Personalization**

   - **AI in Content Creation**: AI generates music, art, and video content, pushing the boundaries of creativity. OpenAI's MuseNet can compose original music in various styles, while AI tools like DeepArt create unique visual artworks.

   - **Personalized Recommendations**: AI algorithms analyze user preferences to provide personalized content recommendations on streaming platforms like Netflix and Spotify, enhancing user experience and engagement.

2. **Interactive Gaming and Virtual Reality**

   - **AI in Gaming**: AI creates intelligent NPCs (non-playable characters) and dynamic game environments, providing immersive and challenging experiences for players. AI-driven game engines like Unity and Unreal Engine incorporate advanced AI techniques.

   - **Virtual Reality (VR) and Augmented Reality (AR)**: AI enhances VR and AR experiences by creating realistic simulations and interactions. Companies like Oculus and Magic Leap use AI to develop immersive virtual environments.

3. **AI in Film and Animation**

   - **AI in Film Production**: AI assists in various aspects of film production, from scriptwriting and editing to visual effects and post-production. Tools like ScriptBook analyze scripts to predict box office success and audience reactions.

   - **Animation and CGI**: AI technologies streamline the animation process and create realistic computer-generated imagery (CGI). Disney Research uses AI to develop advanced animation techniques and improve visual effects.

**Conclusion**

AI is transforming multiple industries by enhancing efficiency, accuracy, and innovation. In healthcare, AI improves diagnostics, personalized treatment, and drug discovery. In finance, AI enhances fraud detection, algorithmic trading, and customer service. Education benefits from personalized learning, AI tutors, and automated grading. Transportation sees advancements in autonomous vehicles, traffic management, and smart logistics. Entertainment is revolutionized by AI-driven content creation, personalized recommendations, and interactive gaming.

As AI continues to evolve, its impact on these industries will only grow, driving further advancements and innovations. Understanding the current trends in AI provides valuable insights into its potential and the opportunities it presents for enhancing various aspects of our lives.

In the following chapters, we will explore AI's integration with other technologies, ethical considerations, and future directions. By building on the knowledge from this chapter, readers will be better equipped to navigate the rapidly evolving landscape of Artificial Intelligence.

# CHAPTER 5: AI AND THE INTERNET OF THINGS (IOT)

**Introduction**

The integration of Artificial Intelligence (AI) with the Internet of Things (IoT) represents a significant advancement in technology, enabling devices to not only connect and communicate but also to learn, adapt, and make intelligent decisions. This chapter explores the synergy between AI and IoT, focusing on smart homes, smart cities, and industrial applications. We will highlight the benefits and challenges associated with this powerful combination.

**The Synergy of AI and IoT**

1. **Defining AI and IoT Integration**
    - **AI in IoT**: AI enhances IoT by providing advanced analytics, learning capabilities, and decision-making processes. This integration enables IoT devices to process large volumes of data, recognize patterns, and make informed decisions without human intervention.
    - **IoT in AI**: IoT provides the data that AI systems need to learn and make decisions. The proliferation of connected devices generates vast amounts of data, which AI algorithms can analyze to derive insights and improve performance.

**Smart Homes**

1. **Intelligent Home Automation**

    ○ **AI-Powered Devices**: Smart home devices such as thermostats, lighting systems, and security cameras use AI to learn user preferences and optimize functionality. For example, the Nest Learning Thermostat uses AI to learn and adapt to the homeowner's schedule, optimizing energy usage.

    ○ **Voice Assistants**: AI-powered voice assistants like Amazon Alexa, Google Assistant, and Apple's Siri control various smart home devices, providing convenience and enhancing user experience.

2. **Energy Efficiency and Cost Savings**

    ○ **Smart Energy Management**: AI algorithms analyze energy consumption patterns and optimize the use of electricity, heating, and cooling systems. Smart meters and AI-driven energy management systems help reduce energy costs and promote sustainability.

    ○ **Predictive Maintenance**: AI detects anomalies and predicts when appliances or systems might fail, allowing for proactive maintenance. This reduces downtime and extends the lifespan of home appliances.

3. **Enhanced Security**

    ○ **AI Security Systems**: Smart security cameras and alarm systems use AI to recognize faces, detect unusual activities, and send alerts to homeowners. Systems like Ring and Arlo provide real-time monitoring and advanced security features.

    ○ **Automated Threat Detection**: AI enhances cybersecurity in smart homes by identifying and mitigating potential threats, such as unauthorized access to IoT devices.

**Smart Cities**

1. **Traffic Management and Transportation**
   - **AI Traffic Control**: AI analyzes real-time traffic data to optimize traffic light timings, reduce congestion, and improve traffic flow. Cities like Los Angeles and Pittsburgh use AI-powered traffic management systems to enhance urban mobility.
   - **Smart Public Transportation**: AI integrates with IoT to monitor and manage public transportation systems, improving efficiency and reducing wait times. Real-time tracking and predictive analytics help optimize bus and train schedules.
2. **Public Safety and Surveillance**
   - **AI Surveillance Systems**: Smart cameras and sensors equipped with AI monitor public spaces, detecting suspicious activities and enhancing security. AI-driven facial recognition systems assist law enforcement in identifying and tracking suspects.
   - **Emergency Response**: AI analyzes data from IoT devices to predict and respond to emergencies such as natural disasters, fires, and medical incidents. Smart city infrastructure includes AI-powered emergency response systems to coordinate rescue efforts.
3. **Environmental Monitoring and Sustainability**
   - **Air Quality Monitoring**: IoT sensors measure air pollution levels, and AI analyzes the data to identify sources of pollution and predict air quality trends. Cities like Beijing use AI to monitor and improve air quality.
   - **Waste Management**: AI optimizes waste collection routes and schedules, reducing operational costs and minimizing environmental impact. Smart bins equipped with sensors provide real-time data on waste levels.

## Industrial Applications

1. **Smart Manufacturing**
   - **Predictive Maintenance**: AI analyzes data from IoT sensors on machinery to predict failures and schedule maintenance before breakdowns occur. This reduces downtime and maintenance costs. Companies like GE and Siemens use AI-driven predictive maintenance in their manufacturing processes.
   - **Quality Control**: AI systems monitor production lines in real-time, identifying defects and ensuring high-quality standards. Vision systems powered by AI detect anomalies in products, enhancing quality control.
2. **Supply Chain Optimization**
   - **Inventory Management**: AI analyzes data from IoT devices to optimize inventory levels, reducing overstock and stockouts. Automated systems manage supply chains more efficiently, improving operational efficiency.
   - **Logistics and Distribution**: AI-powered logistics systems optimize delivery routes, reduce transportation costs, and improve delivery times. Companies like Amazon use AI and IoT to streamline their logistics operations.
3. **Energy Management**
   - **Smart Grids**: AI enhances the management of energy distribution through smart grids, optimizing the balance between energy supply and demand. Smart grids use AI to predict energy consumption patterns and adjust distribution accordingly.
   - **Industrial Energy Efficiency**: AI-driven energy management systems monitor and optimize energy usage in industrial facilities, reducing costs and

environmental impact.

**Benefits of AI and IoT Integration**

1. **Enhanced Decision-Making**
   - **Data-Driven Insights**: AI analyzes data collected from IoT devices to provide actionable insights, improving decision-making processes across various applications.
   - **Real-Time Analytics**: AI processes data in real-time, enabling immediate responses to changing conditions and improving operational efficiency.

2. **Improved Efficiency and Productivity**
   - **Automation**: AI automates routine tasks and processes, increasing efficiency and allowing human workers to focus on more complex and creative tasks.
   - **Optimization**: AI optimizes resource allocation, production processes, and supply chains, reducing waste and increasing productivity.

3. **Cost Savings**
   - **Reduced Operational Costs**: AI-driven predictive maintenance and optimization reduce downtime and maintenance costs, leading to significant savings.
   - **Energy Efficiency**: AI improves energy management, reducing consumption and lowering energy bills.

4. **Enhanced User Experience**
   - **Personalization**: AI personalizes user experiences based on data from IoT devices, providing tailored services and improving customer satisfaction.
   - **Convenience**: Smart home devices and voice assistants enhance convenience, making everyday tasks easier and more efficient.

**Challenges of AI and IoT Integration**

1. **Data Privacy and Security**

- **Privacy Concerns**: The vast amount of data collected by IoT devices raises privacy concerns, as sensitive information could be accessed or misused.
- **Cybersecurity Threats**: IoT devices are often vulnerable to cyberattacks, and securing these devices is crucial to prevent unauthorized access and data breaches.

2. **Interoperability and Standards**

    - **Lack of Standards**: The absence of universal standards for IoT devices and AI systems can lead to compatibility issues and hinder seamless integration.
    - **Integration Challenges**: Ensuring that various IoT devices and AI systems work together harmoniously can be complex and challenging.

3. **Data Management and Processing**

    - **Data Overload**: The sheer volume of data generated by IoT devices can be overwhelming, and managing and processing this data effectively is a significant challenge.
    - **Data Quality**: Ensuring the accuracy and reliability of data collected from IoT devices is essential for AI systems to function correctly.

4. **Cost and Complexity**

    - **Implementation Costs**: The initial investment required for AI and IoT integration can be high, and the complexity of deploying these technologies can be a barrier for some organizations.
    - **Skill Requirements**: Developing and maintaining AI and IoT systems requires specialized skills, and finding qualified professionals can be challenging.

**Conclusion**

The integration of Artificial Intelligence and the Internet of Things offers transformative potential across various domains, from smart homes and cities to industrial applications. The synergy between AI and IoT enhances decision-making, improves efficiency and productivity, and delivers significant cost savings. However, challenges such as data privacy, security, interoperability, and data management must be addressed to fully realize the benefits of this powerful combination.

As AI and IoT technologies continue to evolve, their integration will drive further innovations and improvements in how we live and work. In the next chapters, we will explore other emerging trends in AI, ethical considerations, and future directions. By understanding the current landscape of AI and IoT integration, readers can better appreciate the opportunities and challenges ahead in this dynamic and rapidly changing field.

# CHAPTER 6: BIG DATA AND AI

**Introduction**

Big Data and Artificial Intelligence (AI) are two of the most significant technological advancements of the 21st century. Their synergy has propelled advancements across numerous fields, from healthcare and finance to marketing and manufacturing. This chapter explores the relationship between big data and AI, how data analytics drives AI advancements, and the challenges associated with managing and leveraging big data effectively.

**The Relationship Between Big Data and AI**

1.  **Defining Big Data and AI**
    - **Big Data**: Refers to extremely large datasets that are complex and varied, making traditional data processing techniques inadequate. These datasets are characterized by the four V's: Volume, Variety, Velocity, and Veracity.
    - **Artificial Intelligence**: Refers to the simulation of human intelligence in machines. AI systems can perform tasks such as learning, reasoning, and problem-solving, often using large datasets to improve their accuracy and capabilities.
2.  **How Big Data Fuels AI**
    - **Data-Driven Learning**: AI models, particularly those based on machine learning and deep learning,

require vast amounts of data to train effectively. Big data provides the necessary volume and diversity of information needed for these models to learn patterns, make predictions, and improve over time.

- **Improved Accuracy**: The more data an AI system processes, the more accurately it can perform its tasks. Big data enables AI systems to refine their algorithms, leading to more precise outcomes.
- **Discovery of Insights**: Big data analytics allows AI systems to uncover hidden patterns and correlations that are not immediately obvious. These insights can drive innovation and informed decision-making.

**How Data Analytics Drives AI Advancements**

1. **Machine Learning and Big Data Analytics**
   - **Training Data**: Machine learning algorithms learn from large datasets by identifying patterns and relationships within the data. The availability of big data ensures that these algorithms have enough information to train effectively.
   - **Feature Engineering**: Big data analytics helps in identifying and creating relevant features that improve the performance of machine learning models. By analyzing large datasets, data scientists can derive meaningful features that enhance model accuracy.
   - **Model Evaluation and Tuning**: Big data provides a rich source of validation and testing data, enabling continuous evaluation and fine-tuning of machine learning models to ensure optimal performance.

2. **Deep Learning and Big Data**
   - **Neural Network Training**: Deep learning models, such as convolutional neural networks (CNNs) and recurrent neural networks (RNNs), require extensive datasets to learn complex patterns and representations. Big data is

essential for training these deep neural networks.
- **Natural Language Processing (NLP)**: In NLP applications, big data allows AI systems to understand and generate human language by providing diverse textual data. Large datasets of text enable models like BERT and GPT to perform tasks such as translation, summarization, and sentiment analysis with high accuracy.
- **Image and Video Analysis**: For computer vision tasks, big data comprising millions of images and videos is crucial. Deep learning models trained on these large datasets can perform object detection, facial recognition, and image classification with impressive precision.

3. **Predictive Analytics and Big Data**

   - **Forecasting and Trend Analysis**: Predictive analytics uses historical data to predict future outcomes. Big data enhances the accuracy of these predictions by providing a comprehensive dataset that captures trends and patterns over time.
   - **Anomaly Detection**: AI models use big data to detect anomalies and outliers in various applications, from fraud detection in finance to identifying equipment failures in manufacturing. The extensive datasets allow these models to learn what constitutes normal behavior and identify deviations effectively.

## Applications of Big Data and AI

1. **Healthcare**

   - **Predictive Healthcare**: AI models analyze big data from electronic health records (EHRs), medical imaging, and genomic data to predict disease outbreaks, patient outcomes, and treatment efficacy. IBM Watson Health uses big data and AI to improve cancer diagnosis and

treatment.
- **Personalized Medicine**: Big data analytics enables the development of personalized treatment plans based on a patient's genetic makeup, lifestyle, and medical history. AI systems analyze these large datasets to recommend tailored therapies.

2. **Finance**
   - **Fraud Detection**: AI models analyze transaction data to detect fraudulent activities in real-time. Big data allows these models to learn from a vast number of transactions, improving their ability to identify suspicious patterns.
   - **Algorithmic Trading**: AI-driven trading systems use big data to analyze market trends, historical data, and real-time information to make informed trading decisions. Hedge funds and investment firms leverage big data analytics for high-frequency trading.

3. **Marketing and Customer Insights**
   - **Customer Segmentation**: AI analyzes big data from social media, purchase history, and browsing behavior to segment customers into different groups. This enables personalized marketing strategies and improves customer engagement.
   - **Sentiment Analysis**: AI systems use big data to analyze customer sentiment from reviews, social media posts, and feedback forms. Businesses can use these insights to improve products, services, and customer experiences.

4. **Manufacturing**
   - **Predictive Maintenance**: AI models analyze data from sensors and machinery to predict equipment failures before they occur. This reduces downtime and maintenance costs. Companies like GE and Siemens use

big data and AI for industrial predictive maintenance.

- **Supply Chain Optimization**: Big data analytics enables AI systems to optimize supply chain operations by predicting demand, managing inventory levels, and optimizing logistics. This leads to increased efficiency and cost savings.

5. **Smart Cities**

- **Traffic Management**: AI systems analyze traffic data from sensors, cameras, and GPS devices to optimize traffic flow and reduce congestion. Cities like Los Angeles and Singapore use big data and AI for intelligent traffic management.
- **Energy Management**: AI-driven smart grids use big data to balance energy supply and demand, predict consumption patterns, and optimize energy distribution. This enhances energy efficiency and sustainability in urban areas.

**Challenges Associated with Big Data**

1. **Data Quality and Integrity**

- **Inconsistent Data**: Big data often comes from multiple sources with varying formats and quality. Ensuring data consistency and accuracy is a significant challenge.
- **Data Cleaning**: Cleaning and preprocessing large datasets to remove errors, duplicates, and irrelevant information is time-consuming and resource-intensive.

2. **Data Privacy and Security**

- **Privacy Concerns**: The collection and analysis of large amounts of personal data raise significant privacy concerns. Ensuring compliance with data protection regulations, such as GDPR and CCPA, is crucial.
- **Security Risks**: Big data systems are attractive targets for cyberattacks. Protecting sensitive information from

breaches and unauthorized access is a major challenge.
3. **Scalability and Storage**
       ◦ **Scalability Issues**: Handling and processing vast amounts of data require scalable infrastructure and advanced technologies. Ensuring that systems can scale efficiently with growing data volumes is critical.
       ◦ **Storage Solutions**: Storing massive datasets requires significant storage capacity and efficient data management solutions. Balancing cost, performance, and accessibility is a complex task.
4. **Integration and Interoperability**
       ◦ **Data Integration**: Integrating data from disparate sources, such as sensors, databases, and cloud services, poses significant challenges. Ensuring seamless data integration and interoperability is essential for effective analytics.
       ◦ **Interoperability Standards**: The lack of standardized protocols and formats for big data complicates data sharing and integration. Developing and adhering to interoperability standards is necessary for maximizing the value of big data.
5. **Ethical Considerations**
       ◦ **Bias and Fairness**: AI models trained on biased datasets can perpetuate and amplify existing biases. Ensuring fairness and transparency in AI algorithms is a major ethical concern.
       ◦ **Decision Accountability**: The use of AI for decision-making raises questions about accountability and transparency. Understanding and explaining AI-driven decisions is critical for building trust and ensuring responsible AI use.

**Conclusion**

The relationship between big data and AI is symbiotic, with each technology enhancing the capabilities of the other. Big data provides the vast amounts of information necessary for training AI models, while AI offers advanced analytics and decision-making capabilities to make sense of this data. This synergy drives significant advancements across various industries, from healthcare and finance to marketing and manufacturing.

However, the integration of big data and AI also presents challenges, including data quality, privacy, security, scalability, and ethical considerations. Addressing these challenges is crucial for leveraging the full potential of big data and AI.

In the following chapters, we will explore other emerging trends in AI, including its integration with other technologies, ethical considerations, and future directions. By understanding the current landscape of big data and AI, readers can better appreciate the opportunities and challenges ahead in this dynamic and rapidly evolving field.

# CHAPTER 7: AI IN BUSINESS AND INDUSTRY

**Introduction**

Artificial Intelligence (AI) is transforming business and industry by enhancing efficiency, improving decision-making, and creating new opportunities for growth. This chapter explores how businesses leverage AI in various domains, including customer service, marketing, sales, supply chain management, and human resources. Through case studies and examples, we will illustrate the practical applications and benefits of AI in these areas.

**AI in Customer Service**

1. **AI-Powered Chatbots and Virtual Assistants**
    - **Overview**: AI-driven chatbots and virtual assistants handle customer inquiries, provide support, and guide users through processes, offering 24/7 service and improving customer satisfaction.
    - **Case Study: Bank of America's Erica**: Erica is an AI virtual assistant that helps customers with banking tasks, such as checking balances, transferring money, and providing financial advice. Erica uses natural language processing (NLP) to understand and respond to customer queries, enhancing user experience.
2. **Sentiment Analysis and Feedback Management**

- **Overview**: AI analyzes customer feedback from various channels (social media, reviews, surveys) to gauge sentiment and identify areas for improvement.
- **Case Study: Hootsuite**: Hootsuite uses AI for sentiment analysis to monitor social media conversations. The insights gained help businesses understand customer sentiment and respond appropriately, improving customer relations.

3. **Automated Customer Support Systems**
   - **Overview**: AI systems automate repetitive customer support tasks, such as password resets and order tracking, freeing up human agents for more complex issues.
   - **Case Study: Zendesk**: Zendesk's AI-driven customer support platform uses machine learning to classify and prioritize tickets, providing faster and more efficient service.

**AI in Marketing**

1. **Personalized Marketing Campaigns**
   - **Overview**: AI analyzes customer data to create personalized marketing campaigns, targeting individuals with relevant content and offers.
   - **Case Study: Netflix**: Netflix uses AI to recommend personalized content to users based on their viewing history and preferences. This personalization increases user engagement and retention.

2. **Predictive Analytics for Market Trends**
   - **Overview**: AI uses predictive analytics to identify market trends and consumer behavior, enabling businesses to make data-driven marketing decisions.
   - **Case Study: Coca-Cola**: Coca-Cola uses AI-driven predictive analytics to optimize its marketing strategies, identifying emerging trends and tailoring

campaigns to target specific demographics.
3. **Dynamic Pricing Strategies**
    - **Overview**: AI systems adjust prices in real-time based on demand, competitor pricing, and other factors, maximizing revenue and competitiveness.
    - **Case Study: Amazon**: Amazon employs AI-powered dynamic pricing to adjust product prices based on market conditions, customer behavior, and inventory levels, ensuring competitive pricing and increased sales.

## AI in Sales

1. **Sales Forecasting and Lead Scoring**
    - **Overview**: AI models analyze historical sales data and customer interactions to forecast future sales and score leads based on their likelihood to convert.
    - **Case Study: Salesforce Einstein**: Salesforce Einstein uses AI to provide predictive lead scoring and sales forecasting, helping sales teams prioritize high-potential leads and improve sales outcomes.
2. **Automated Sales Assistants**
    - **Overview**: AI-powered sales assistants handle routine tasks, such as scheduling meetings, sending follow-up emails, and updating CRM systems, allowing sales teams to focus on closing deals.
    - **Case Study: X.ai**: X.ai's AI assistant, Amy, schedules meetings and manages calendars for sales teams, reducing administrative burden and improving productivity.
3. **Customer Relationship Management (CRM)**
    - **Overview**: AI-enhanced CRM systems analyze customer data to provide insights and recommendations for building stronger customer relationships and increasing sales.
    - **Case Study: HubSpot**: HubSpot's AI-driven CRM

platform uses machine learning to analyze customer interactions, providing actionable insights for sales teams to enhance customer engagement and drive sales.

## AI in Supply Chain Management

1. **Inventory Optimization**

   - **Overview**: AI analyzes sales data, market trends, and inventory levels to optimize stock levels, reducing overstock and stockouts.
   - **Case Study: Walmart**: Walmart uses AI to manage its vast inventory across numerous stores, predicting demand and optimizing stock levels to ensure product availability and reduce excess inventory.

2. **Demand Forecasting**

   - **Overview**: AI models predict future demand for products based on historical data, market trends, and external factors, enabling businesses to plan and allocate resources effectively.
   - **Case Study: Amazon**: Amazon employs AI-driven demand forecasting to anticipate customer needs and manage inventory, ensuring timely delivery and high customer satisfaction.

3. **Logistics and Route Optimization**

   - **Overview**: AI optimizes logistics and transportation routes, reducing delivery times, fuel consumption, and operational costs.
   - **Case Study: UPS**: UPS's ORION (On-Road Integrated Optimization and Navigation) system uses AI to optimize delivery routes, saving millions of miles and gallons of fuel annually.

## AI in Human Resources

1. **Talent Acquisition and Recruitment**

- **Overview**: AI streamlines the recruitment process by analyzing resumes, conducting initial interviews, and identifying the best candidates based on predefined criteria.
- **Case Study: LinkedIn Talent Insights**: LinkedIn's AI-driven talent acquisition tool analyzes data from millions of profiles to help recruiters identify and engage with top talent.

2. **Employee Performance Management**

   - **Overview**: AI monitors employee performance, providing real-time feedback and identifying areas for improvement. It also predicts potential attrition and suggests retention strategies.
   - **Case Study: IBM Watson**: IBM Watson uses AI to analyze employee data, providing insights into performance, engagement, and potential risks, helping HR teams manage talent more effectively.

3. **Training and Development**

   - **Overview**: AI personalizes employee training programs by analyzing individual learning styles, performance metrics, and career goals, ensuring targeted and effective development.
   - **Case Study: Coursera for Business**: Coursera's AI-driven platform offers personalized training recommendations based on employee skills and career aspirations, enhancing workforce development.

## Case Studies and Examples

1. **AI in Retail: H&M**

   - **Overview**: H&M uses AI to analyze customer data, manage inventory, and optimize pricing strategies. By leveraging AI, H&M can predict fashion trends, personalize marketing campaigns, and ensure efficient stock management.

- **Benefits**: Increased sales, reduced inventory costs, and improved customer satisfaction.

2. **AI in Banking: JPMorgan Chase**
   - **Overview**: JPMorgan Chase employs AI for fraud detection, risk management, and customer service. The bank's COiN (Contract Intelligence) platform uses AI to review legal documents, saving thousands of hours of manual work.
   - **Benefits**: Enhanced security, reduced operational costs, and improved efficiency.

3. **AI in Manufacturing: Siemens**
   - **Overview**: Siemens uses AI to optimize manufacturing processes, predict equipment failures, and enhance product quality. The company's AI-driven MindSphere platform collects and analyzes data from industrial machines, enabling predictive maintenance and process optimization.
   - **Benefits**: Reduced downtime, increased productivity, and improved product quality.

4. **AI in Healthcare: Mayo Clinic**
   - **Overview**: Mayo Clinic uses AI to analyze patient data, predict disease outcomes, and personalize treatment plans. AI-driven diagnostic tools assist doctors in making accurate diagnoses and recommending effective treatments.
   - **Benefits**: Improved patient outcomes, enhanced diagnostic accuracy, and personalized care.

5. **AI in Transportation: Uber**
   - **Overview**: Uber employs AI for route optimization, demand prediction, and dynamic pricing. The company's AI algorithms analyze real-time data to match drivers with passengers, optimize routes, and adjust prices based on demand and supply.
   - **Benefits**: Reduced wait times, increased efficiency, and

optimized pricing.

**Conclusion**

AI is transforming business and industry by enhancing efficiency, improving decision-making, and driving innovation across various domains, including customer service, marketing, sales, supply chain management, and human resources. Through the use of AI-powered tools and platforms, businesses can streamline operations, personalize customer experiences, and gain a competitive edge.

The case studies and examples provided in this chapter illustrate the practical applications and benefits of AI in different industries. As AI technology continues to evolve, its impact on business and industry will only grow, creating new opportunities and challenges.

In the following chapters, we will explore other emerging trends in AI, ethical considerations, and future directions. By understanding the current landscape of AI in business and industry, readers can better appreciate the opportunities and challenges ahead in this dynamic and rapidly evolving field.

# CHAPTER 8: AI AND AUTOMATION

**Introduction**

Artificial Intelligence (AI) and automation are revolutionizing industries by streamlining processes, enhancing efficiency, and reducing costs. This chapter highlights the role of AI in robotics, autonomous vehicles, and manufacturing. We will explore the benefits and potential disruptions caused by automation, providing a comprehensive overview of its impact on the modern world.

**AI in Robotics**

1. **Industrial Robotics**
    - **Overview**: Industrial robots, powered by AI, are designed to perform repetitive and hazardous tasks with precision and speed. These robots are commonly used in manufacturing, assembly lines, and logistics.
    - **Case Study: Fanuc**: Fanuc, a leading manufacturer of industrial robots, uses AI to enable robots to learn from their environment and improve their performance over time. These robots are employed in tasks such as welding, painting, and material handling.
    - **Benefits**: Increased productivity, improved product quality, reduced human error, and enhanced workplace safety.
2. **Service Robotics**

CHAPTER 8: AI AND AUTOMATION | 45

- **Overview**: Service robots, equipped with AI, assist in various sectors such as healthcare, hospitality, and retail. These robots interact with humans and perform tasks like customer service, cleaning, and delivery.
- **Case Study: SoftBank Robotics 'Pepper**: Pepper, an AI-powered humanoid robot, is used in retail and hospitality to greet customers, provide information, and enhance customer experiences.
- **Benefits**: Improved customer service, efficient task automation, and enhanced user experiences.

3. **Collaborative Robots (Cobots)**

    - **Overview**: Cobots are designed to work alongside humans, assisting in tasks that require human-robot collaboration. AI enables cobots to learn from human actions and adapt to dynamic environments.
    - **Case Study: Universal Robots**: Universal Robots' cobots are used in various industries for tasks such as assembly, packaging, and quality inspection. These robots are designed to be safe and easy to program.
    - **Benefits**: Increased flexibility, enhanced human-robot collaboration, and improved efficiency.

## AI in Autonomous Vehicles

1. **Self-Driving Cars**

    - **Overview**: Autonomous vehicles, powered by AI, are capable of navigating and driving without human intervention. AI algorithms process data from sensors, cameras, and GPS to make real-time driving decisions.
    - **Case Study: Waymo**: Waymo, a subsidiary of Alphabet, has developed self-driving technology that enables vehicles to operate autonomously. Waymo's autonomous vehicles are being tested and deployed in various locations for ride-hailing services.
    - **Benefits**: Improved road safety, reduced traffic congestion, and increased mobility for individuals who

cannot drive.

2. **AI in Fleet Management**
   - **Overview**: AI is used in fleet management to optimize routes, monitor vehicle performance, and predict maintenance needs. This enhances the efficiency and reliability of transportation fleets.
   - **Case Study: UPS**: UPS uses AI-powered ORION (On-Road Integrated Optimization and Navigation) to optimize delivery routes, reducing fuel consumption and improving delivery times.
   - **Benefits**: Reduced operational costs, improved delivery efficiency, and enhanced customer satisfaction.

3. **Advanced Driver Assistance Systems (ADAS)**
   - **Overview**: ADAS are AI-powered systems that assist drivers by providing real-time information, warnings, and automated actions to enhance driving safety. These systems include features like lane-keeping assist, adaptive cruise control, and collision avoidance.
   - **Case Study: Tesla Autopilot**: Tesla's Autopilot system uses AI to provide semi-autonomous driving capabilities, enhancing driver safety and convenience.
   - **Benefits**: Enhanced driver safety, reduced risk of accidents, and improved driving comfort.

## AI in Manufacturing

1. **Smart Manufacturing**
   - **Overview**: AI-driven smart manufacturing leverages advanced technologies such as IoT, machine learning, and robotics to optimize production processes, improve product quality, and reduce costs.
   - **Case Study: Siemens 'MindSphere**: MindSphere, Siemens 'cloud-based IoT operating system, uses AI to collect and analyze data from industrial machines, enabling predictive maintenance

and process optimization.
   - **Benefits**: Increased production efficiency, reduced downtime, and improved product quality.
2. **Predictive Maintenance**
   - **Overview**: AI-powered predictive maintenance uses data from sensors and machines to predict equipment failures and schedule maintenance before issues arise. This minimizes downtime and extends the lifespan of machinery.
   - **Case Study: GE's Predix**: GE's Predix platform uses AI to monitor and analyze data from industrial equipment, predicting maintenance needs and preventing unexpected failures.
   - **Benefits**: Reduced maintenance costs, minimized downtime, and extended equipment lifespan.
3. **Quality Control and Inspection**
   - **Overview**: AI enhances quality control by automating the inspection process and detecting defects in real-time. Computer vision and machine learning algorithms analyze product images and identify anomalies.
   - **Case Study: FANUC's Zero Down Time (ZDT)**: FANUC's ZDT system uses AI to monitor and analyze the performance of robotic systems, identifying potential issues and ensuring consistent product quality.
   - **Benefits**: Improved product quality, reduced waste, and enhanced production efficiency.

## Benefits of AI and Automation

1. **Increased Efficiency and Productivity**
   - **Automation of Repetitive Tasks**: AI automates repetitive and mundane tasks, allowing human workers to focus on more complex and creative activities. This leads to increased efficiency and productivity.

- **Optimized Resource Utilization**: AI optimizes the use of resources such as energy, materials, and labor, reducing costs and maximizing output.

2. **Enhanced Accuracy and Consistency**
   - **Reduced Human Error**: AI systems perform tasks with high accuracy and consistency, minimizing the risk of errors and improving overall quality.
   - **Data-Driven Decision Making**: AI analyzes large volumes of data to provide insights and recommendations, enabling informed and data-driven decision-making.

3. **Cost Savings**
   - **Lower Operational Costs**: Automation reduces labor costs and operational expenses by streamlining processes and improving efficiency.
   - **Predictive Maintenance**: AI-driven predictive maintenance reduces maintenance costs and prevents costly downtime by identifying potential issues before they become critical.

4. **Improved Safety**
   - **Hazardous Task Automation**: AI-powered robots and autonomous systems perform hazardous tasks, reducing the risk of injuries and accidents in the workplace.
   - **Enhanced Workplace Safety**: AI monitors and analyzes safety conditions, ensuring compliance with safety regulations and preventing accidents.

**Potential Disruptions Caused by Automation**

1. **Job Displacement and Workforce Challenges**
   - **Job Losses**: Automation may lead to job displacement as machines and AI systems take over tasks traditionally performed by human workers. This is particularly impactful in industries reliant on repetitive and manual

labor.
- **Skills Gap**: The shift towards automation creates a demand for new skills, such as AI programming and robotics, leading to a skills gap in the workforce. Workers need to adapt and acquire new skills to remain relevant in the job market.

2. **Economic and Social Impact**
   - **Economic Inequality**: Automation may exacerbate economic inequality as high-skilled workers benefit from new opportunities, while low-skilled workers face job losses and reduced income prospects.
   - **Social Disruption**: The transition to an automated economy can cause social disruption, with communities dependent on traditional industries experiencing economic decline and reduced social cohesion.

3. **Ethical and Legal Considerations**
   - **Accountability and Liability**: The deployment of autonomous systems raises questions about accountability and liability in case of accidents or malfunctions. Determining responsibility for AI-driven decisions is a complex legal and ethical challenge.
   - **Privacy Concerns**: AI systems that collect and analyze data raise concerns about data privacy and security. Ensuring that personal data is protected and used ethically is crucial.

4. **Technological Dependence**
   - **Over-Reliance on Automation**: Excessive reliance on automated systems may lead to vulnerabilities, such as system failures and cybersecurity risks. Maintaining a balance between automation and human oversight is essential.
   - **Resilience and Adaptability**: Organizations must ensure that their workforce and systems are adaptable

and resilient to technological changes and disruptions.

## Conclusion

AI and automation are transforming robotics, autonomous vehicles, and manufacturing by enhancing efficiency, improving accuracy, and reducing costs. While the benefits of automation are significant, including increased productivity, cost savings, and improved safety, it also poses challenges such as job displacement, economic inequality, and ethical concerns.

Understanding the role of AI in automation and addressing the associated challenges is essential for maximizing its potential and ensuring a balanced and inclusive approach to technological advancement. In the following chapters, we will explore other emerging trends in AI, ethical considerations, and future directions. By comprehending the current landscape of AI and automation, readers can better navigate the opportunities and challenges ahead in this dynamic and rapidly evolving field.

# CHAPTER 9:
# ETHICS AND AI

**Introduction**

As Artificial Intelligence (AI) continues to advance and integrate into various aspects of society, its ethical implications have become a critical area of concern. This chapter examines the ethical considerations surrounding AI, including privacy concerns, bias, fairness, and regulatory challenges. We will also discuss the importance of developing ethical AI practices to ensure responsible and equitable use of this transformative technology.

**Privacy Concerns**

1. **Data Collection and Consent**
    - **Overview**: AI systems often rely on vast amounts of data to function effectively. This data is collected from various sources, including personal devices, social media, and public records. The collection and use of personal data raise significant privacy concerns, particularly regarding user consent and awareness.
    - **Case Study: Facebook-Cambridge Analytica Scandal**: In 2018, it was revealed that Cambridge Analytica had harvested the personal data of millions of Facebook users without their consent to influence political campaigns. This scandal highlighted the potential for misuse of personal data and the need for stricter privacy protections.

- **Ethical Considerations**: Ensuring that individuals are fully informed about the data being collected and how it will be used is crucial. Implementing transparent data collection practices and obtaining explicit consent from users can help mitigate privacy concerns.

2. **Data Security and Protection**

    - **Overview**: The vast amounts of data collected and stored by AI systems make them attractive targets for cyberattacks. Data breaches can expose sensitive information, leading to identity theft, financial loss, and other harms.
    - **Case Study: Equifax Data Breach**: In 2017, credit reporting agency Equifax suffered a data breach that exposed the personal information of 147 million people. This incident underscored the importance of robust data security measures.
    - **Ethical Considerations**: Organizations must implement strong security protocols to protect data from unauthorized access and cyberattacks. Ensuring data integrity and confidentiality is essential for maintaining user trust.

## Bias and Fairness

1. **Algorithmic Bias**

    - **Overview**: AI systems can inadvertently perpetuate or even amplify existing biases present in the data they are trained on. Bias in AI algorithms can lead to unfair and discriminatory outcomes, particularly in areas such as hiring, lending, and law enforcement.
    - **Case Study: Amazon's Recruiting Tool**: In 2018, Amazon abandoned an AI recruiting tool that was found to be biased against women. The tool had been trained on resumes submitted over a 10-year period, most of which came from men, leading the algorithm to favor male candidates.

- **Ethical Considerations**: Addressing algorithmic bias requires diverse and representative training data, continuous monitoring for biased outcomes, and transparent algorithmic design. Implementing fairness audits and bias mitigation strategies can help create more equitable AI systems.

2. **Fairness and Discrimination**
    - **Overview**: Ensuring fairness in AI systems involves creating algorithms that provide equal treatment and opportunities to all individuals, regardless of race, gender, socioeconomic status, or other characteristics. Discriminatory practices in AI can have far-reaching consequences, perpetuating social inequalities.
    - **Case Study: COMPAS Recidivism Algorithm**: The COMPAS algorithm, used in the U.S. criminal justice system to predict recidivism, was found to disproportionately assign higher risk scores to African American defendants compared to white defendants. This raised concerns about racial discrimination in AI-driven decision-making.
    - **Ethical Considerations**: Developing fair AI systems requires a commitment to diversity and inclusion throughout the AI lifecycle. Regularly assessing algorithms for discriminatory impacts and involving diverse stakeholders in the development process can promote fairness.

## Regulatory Challenges

1. **Lack of Standardized Regulations**
    - **Overview**: The rapid advancement of AI technology has outpaced the development of comprehensive regulatory frameworks. The lack of standardized regulations poses challenges in ensuring consistent and ethical AI practices across different regions and industries.

- **Case Study: European Union's AI Act**: The European Union is working on an AI Act to establish a legal framework for AI, focusing on high-risk applications and ensuring transparency, accountability, and human oversight. This initiative aims to set a global standard for AI regulation.
- **Ethical Considerations**: Governments and regulatory bodies must collaborate to create harmonized AI regulations that address ethical concerns while fostering innovation. Establishing clear guidelines and standards can help ensure responsible AI development and deployment.

2. **Enforcement and Accountability**

    - **Overview**: Effective enforcement of AI regulations requires mechanisms to hold organizations accountable for their AI systems 'ethical and legal compliance. Ensuring accountability is crucial for addressing ethical breaches and maintaining public trust.
    - **Case Study: General Data Protection Regulation (GDPR)**: The GDPR, implemented by the European Union in 2018, is a comprehensive data protection regulation that includes provisions for AI. It mandates transparency, user consent, and data protection, with significant penalties for non-compliance.
    - **Ethical Considerations**: Establishing enforcement bodies and accountability measures, such as regular audits and impact assessments, can help ensure that AI systems adhere to ethical standards. Encouraging organizations to adopt ethical guidelines and best practices is essential for responsible AI use.

**Importance of Developing Ethical AI Practices**

1. **Building Trust and Transparency**

    - **Overview**: Transparent AI systems foster trust among users and stakeholders by providing clear information about how AI decisions are made. Transparency involves explaining the data sources, algorithms, and decision-making processes used by AI systems.

- **Ethical Considerations**: Developing explainable AI (XAI) techniques can help make AI systems more transparent and understandable. Organizations should prioritize transparency to build trust and ensure accountability.

2. **Promoting Inclusivity and Diversity**

   - **Overview**: Inclusive and diverse AI development practices ensure that AI systems are designed to meet the needs of all users, avoiding biases and discrimination. Involving diverse perspectives in the AI development process can lead to more equitable outcomes.
   - **Ethical Considerations**: Encouraging diversity in AI research and development teams and engaging with marginalized communities can help create more inclusive AI systems. Promoting diversity in data collection and algorithm design is crucial for reducing bias.

3. **Ensuring Accountability and Governance**

   - **Overview**: Establishing governance frameworks for AI involves setting ethical guidelines, standards, and best practices that organizations must follow. Accountability mechanisms ensure that organizations are responsible for their AI systems 'ethical and legal compliance.
   - **Ethical Considerations**: Developing ethical AI frameworks, such as the IEEE Global Initiative on Ethics of Autonomous and Intelligent Systems, can provide valuable guidance for responsible AI use. Organizations should adopt these frameworks and implement robust governance structures.

4. **Fostering Collaboration and Education**

- **Overview**: Collaboration between governments, industry, academia, and civil society is essential for addressing the ethical challenges of AI. Education and awareness initiatives can help stakeholders understand the ethical implications of AI and promote responsible practices.
- **Ethical Considerations**: Creating multidisciplinary forums and working groups to discuss AI ethics can foster collaboration and innovation. Educational programs and public awareness campaigns can raise understanding of AI ethics and encourage responsible AI use.

## Conclusion

The ethical implications of AI are multifaceted, encompassing privacy concerns, bias, fairness, and regulatory challenges. As AI continues to advance and permeate various aspects of society, addressing these ethical considerations is paramount to ensuring responsible and equitable AI development and deployment.

Developing ethical AI practices involves building trust and transparency, promoting inclusivity and diversity, ensuring accountability and governance, and fostering collaboration and education. By prioritizing ethical considerations, organizations and stakeholders can harness the transformative potential of AI while mitigating its risks and ensuring that its benefits are distributed equitably.

In the following chapters, we will explore other emerging trends in AI and its future directions. By understanding the ethical landscape of AI, readers can better navigate the opportunities and challenges ahead in this dynamic and rapidly evolving field.

# CHAPTER 10: FUTURE TRENDS IN AI

**Introduction**

Artificial Intelligence (AI) continues to evolve at a rapid pace, pushing the boundaries of what technology can achieve. This chapter explores some of the most exciting and transformative future trends in AI, including quantum computing, AI in space exploration, predictive analytics, and blockchain integration. By understanding these emerging trends, we can better anticipate the future landscape of AI and its potential impact on various industries and aspects of society.

**Quantum Computing and AI**

1. **Overview of Quantum Computing**
   - **Definition**: Quantum computing leverages the principles of quantum mechanics to process information in ways that classical computers cannot. Quantum bits, or qubits, can exist in multiple states simultaneously, allowing for parallel computations and potentially solving complex problems more efficiently.
   - **Potential Impact on AI**: Quantum computing could revolutionize AI by significantly speeding up data processing, enhancing machine learning algorithms, and enabling the handling of massive datasets more efficiently.
2. **Applications of Quantum Computing in AI**

- **Optimization Problems**: Quantum computers can solve optimization problems much faster than classical computers. This has applications in various fields, including logistics, finance, and material science.
- **Drug Discovery**: Quantum computing can simulate molecular structures and interactions at an unprecedented scale, accelerating drug discovery and development.
- **Machine Learning**: Quantum machine learning algorithms could outperform classical algorithms in tasks such as pattern recognition, data classification, and clustering.

3. **Case Study: Google's Quantum Supremacy**

    - **Overview**: In 2019, Google announced that its quantum computer, Sycamore, had achieved quantum supremacy by performing a complex calculation in 200 seconds that would take a classical supercomputer thousands of years.
    - **Implications**: This milestone demonstrates the potential of quantum computing to revolutionize AI and other fields, paving the way for more advanced and efficient AI systems.

## AI in Space Exploration

1. **Overview of AI in Space Exploration**

    - **Definition**: AI is increasingly being used in space missions to enhance the capabilities of spacecraft, improve mission planning, and analyze vast amounts of data collected from space.
    - **Potential Impact**: AI can improve the efficiency and safety of space missions, enable autonomous operations, and facilitate the discovery of new celestial phenomena.

2. **Applications of AI in Space Exploration**

- **Autonomous Spacecraft Navigation**: AI enables spacecraft to navigate autonomously, avoiding obstacles and making real-time decisions during missions.
- **Rover Operations**: AI-powered rovers, such as NASA's Perseverance, use machine learning algorithms to analyze terrain, identify scientific targets, and perform autonomous exploration.
- **Data Analysis**: AI analyzes data from telescopes and space probes to identify celestial objects, detect exoplanets, and study cosmic phenomena.

3. **Case Study: NASA's Perseverance Rover**
   - **Overview**: NASA's Perseverance Rover, which landed on Mars in 2021, uses AI to navigate the Martian surface, conduct scientific experiments, and search for signs of past life.
   - **Implications**: The use of AI in the Perseverance mission demonstrates how AI can enhance the capabilities of space exploration, enabling more complex and autonomous missions in the future.

## Predictive Analytics

1. **Overview of Predictive Analytics**
   - **Definition**: Predictive analytics uses statistical algorithms and machine learning techniques to analyze historical data and make predictions about future events and trends.
   - **Potential Impact**: Predictive analytics can transform various industries by providing actionable insights, improving decision-making, and enabling proactive strategies.

2. **Applications of Predictive Analytics**
   - **Healthcare**: Predictive analytics can forecast disease outbreaks, predict patient outcomes, and personalize

treatment plans.
- **Finance**: AI models analyze market trends and economic indicators to predict stock prices, assess credit risk, and detect fraud.
- **Retail**: Retailers use predictive analytics to forecast demand, optimize inventory levels, and personalize marketing campaigns.

3. **Case Study: IBM Watson Health**
   - **Overview**: IBM Watson Health uses predictive analytics to analyze patient data and predict disease progression, enabling personalized treatment plans and improving patient outcomes.
   - **Implications**: The success of IBM Watson Health demonstrates the potential of predictive analytics to revolutionize healthcare and other industries by providing accurate and actionable insights.

## Blockchain Integration

1. **Overview of Blockchain and AI Integration**
   - **Definition**: Blockchain is a decentralized ledger technology that ensures data integrity and security. Integrating AI with blockchain can enhance the transparency, security, and trustworthiness of AI systems.
   - **Potential Impact**: Blockchain integration can address some of the key challenges in AI, such as data privacy, security, and ethical concerns.

2. **Applications of Blockchain Integration in AI**
   - **Data Security and Privacy**: Blockchain can secure data used by AI systems, ensuring that it is tamper-proof and only accessible to authorized parties.
   - **Decentralized AI**: Blockchain enables the development of decentralized AI models, where data and computational resources are distributed across

a network, reducing the risk of data breaches and centralization.
    - **Transparent AI Models**: Blockchain can create an immutable record of AI model decisions and data sources, enhancing transparency and accountability.
3. **Case Study: SingularityNET**
    - **Overview**: SingularityNET is a decentralized AI platform that uses blockchain to enable AI developers to share and monetize their AI models and datasets securely.
    - **Implications**: The success of SingularityNET demonstrates how blockchain integration can facilitate the development and deployment of AI in a secure and transparent manner, promoting collaboration and innovation.

## Other Emerging Trends in AI

1. **Edge AI**
    - **Overview**: Edge AI refers to deploying AI algorithms on edge devices (e.g., smartphones, IoT devices) rather than relying on centralized cloud computing. This enables real-time data processing and decision-making at the source of data generation.
    - **Applications**: Edge AI is used in autonomous vehicles, smart cameras, and wearable devices to provide real-time insights and enhance performance.
    - **Benefits**: Reduced latency, enhanced data privacy, and improved efficiency.
2. **Explainable AI (XAI)**
    - **Overview**: Explainable AI focuses on developing AI models that are transparent and interpretable, enabling users to understand how decisions are made.
    - **Applications**: XAI is critical in healthcare, finance, and legal sectors, where understanding AI decisions is

essential for trust and compliance.
- **Benefits**: Increased transparency, improved trust, and enhanced accountability.

3. **AI Ethics and Governance**
    - **Overview**: As AI becomes more pervasive, there is a growing focus on establishing ethical guidelines and governance frameworks to ensure responsible AI development and deployment.
    - **Applications**: AI ethics initiatives are being implemented in various sectors to address issues such as bias, fairness, and accountability.
    - **Benefits**: Promotes ethical AI use, mitigates risks, and fosters public trust.

4. **AI in Creative Industries**
    - **Overview**: AI is increasingly being used in creative industries such as art, music, and literature to generate new content and enhance creative processes.
    - **Applications**: AI-generated art, music composition, and automated content creation are becoming more prevalent.
    - **Benefits**: Fosters innovation, enhances creativity, and provides new tools for artists and creators.

**Conclusion**

The future of AI is marked by exciting and transformative trends that have the potential to revolutionize various industries and aspects of society. Quantum computing promises to enhance AI capabilities, while AI in space exploration enables more autonomous and complex missions. Predictive analytics provides actionable insights across different sectors, and blockchain integration addresses key challenges in AI, such as security and transparency.

Additionally, emerging trends such as edge AI, explainable AI, AI ethics and governance, and AI in creative industries highlight the diverse applications and opportunities that lie ahead. By staying informed about these future trends, organizations and individuals can better navigate the rapidly evolving landscape of AI and harness its full potential for innovation and growth.

In the following chapters, we will explore the practical implementation of AI in various domains, case studies of successful AI applications, and strategies for developing and deploying AI responsibly. By understanding the future trends in AI, readers can better prepare for the opportunities and challenges that lie ahead in this dynamic and rapidly evolving field.

# CHAPTER 11: AI TOOLS AND PLATFORMS

**Introduction**

The development and deployment of Artificial Intelligence (AI) applications have been greatly facilitated by a variety of tools, platforms, and services. These resources provide the necessary infrastructure, frameworks, and algorithms to create, train, and deploy AI models efficiently. This chapter introduces popular AI development tools, cloud AI services, and open-source platforms, discussing their features and applications.

**AI Development Tools**

1. **TensorFlow**
    - **Overview**: TensorFlow is an open-source machine learning framework developed by Google. It is widely used for building and deploying machine learning models, particularly deep learning applications.
    - **Features**:
        - Comprehensive ecosystem including TensorFlow Lite for mobile and embedded devices, TensorFlow.js for JavaScript development, and TensorFlow Extended (TFX) for production ML pipelines.
        - Support for various data types and models, including neural networks, reinforcement learning, and generative models.
        - Strong community support and extensive

documentation.
- **Applications**: TensorFlow is used in diverse fields such as natural language processing (NLP), computer vision, speech recognition, and recommendation systems.

2. **PyTorch**
   - **Overview**: PyTorch is an open-source machine learning library developed by Facebook's AI Research lab. It is known for its dynamic computation graph and ease of use, making it popular among researchers and developers.
   - **Features**:
     - Dynamic computation graph that allows for more flexible model building and debugging.
     - Integration with Python, providing seamless integration with Python libraries like NumPy and SciPy.
     - Support for distributed training and production deployment through TorchServe.
   - **Applications**: PyTorch is used in academic research, deep learning, reinforcement learning, and computer vision projects.

3. **Keras**
   - **Overview**: Keras is a high-level neural networks API, written in Python and capable of running on top of TensorFlow, Theano, and Microsoft Cognitive Toolkit (CNTK). It focuses on enabling fast experimentation.
   - **Features**:
     - User-friendly and modular API that simplifies building and training neural networks.
     - Integration with TensorFlow 2.0, making it easier to scale and deploy models.
     - Pre-trained models and layers available for quick development.
   - **Applications**: Keras is widely used in educational settings, prototyping, and production-scale

deep learning applications.

4. **Scikit-learn**
    - **Overview**: Scikit-learn is an open-source machine learning library for Python, built on NumPy, SciPy, and Matplotlib. It provides simple and efficient tools for data analysis and modeling.
    - **Features**:
        - Extensive collection of machine learning algorithms for classification, regression, clustering, and dimensionality reduction.
        - Tools for model evaluation, hyperparameter tuning, and pipeline creation.
        - Well-documented and easy to use, making it accessible for beginners and experts alike.
    - **Applications**: Scikit-learn is used for data mining, data analysis, and building machine learning models in various industries.

**Cloud AI Services**

1. **Google Cloud AI**
    - **Overview**: Google Cloud AI offers a suite of machine learning services and tools on Google Cloud Platform, enabling developers to build, train, and deploy models at scale.
    - **Features**:
        - AutoML: Automated machine learning services for building high-quality models with minimal effort.
        - AI Platform: Managed services for training, deploying, and managing machine learning models.
        - Pre-trained APIs: APIs for natural language processing, computer vision, translation, and more.
    - **Applications**: Google Cloud AI is used in industries such

as healthcare, finance, retail, and telecommunications for tasks like image recognition, natural language understanding, and predictive analytics.

2. **Amazon Web Services (AWS) AI**
   - **Overview**: AWS AI provides a range of AI and machine learning services on Amazon Web Services, offering scalable and flexible solutions for developers.
   - **Features**:
     - SageMaker: A fully managed service for building, training, and deploying machine learning models.
     - AI Services: Pre-trained services for tasks like text-to-speech (Amazon Polly), image and video analysis (Amazon Rekognition), and natural language processing (Amazon Comprehend).
     - Machine Learning Infrastructure: High-performance computing and storage options for large-scale machine learning workloads.
   - **Applications**: AWS AI is used in e-commerce, healthcare, finance, and manufacturing for applications such as personalized recommendations, fraud detection, and predictive maintenance.

3. **Microsoft Azure AI**
   - **Overview**: Microsoft Azure AI offers a comprehensive set of AI services and tools on Microsoft Azure, supporting the entire machine learning lifecycle.
   - **Features**:
     - Azure Machine Learning: A platform for building, training, and deploying machine learning models with integrated DevOps.
     - Cognitive Services: APIs for vision, speech, language, and decision-making capabilities.
     - Bot Services: Tools for building and deploying intelligent bots across various channels.
   - **Applications**: Azure AI is used in sectors such as healthcare, finance, retail, and government

for solutions like medical imaging, customer service automation, and predictive analytics.

## Open-Source AI Platforms

1. **Apache Spark**
   - **Overview**: Apache Spark is an open-source unified analytics engine for big data processing, with built-in modules for streaming, SQL, machine learning, and graph processing.
   - **Features**:
     - Scalable and fast data processing engine for large-scale data analytics.
     - MLlib: A scalable machine learning library integrated with Spark for building and deploying machine learning models.
     - Support for various programming languages, including Python, Java, Scala, and R.
   - **Applications**: Apache Spark is used in data analytics, real-time data processing, machine learning, and big data applications across industries such as finance, healthcare, and telecommunications.

2. **H2O.ai**
   - **Overview**: H2O.ai is an open-source machine learning and artificial intelligence platform that provides tools for building and deploying machine learning models.
   - **Features**:
     - H2O-3: An open-source platform for distributed in-memory machine learning, supporting various algorithms.
     - Driverless AI: An automated machine learning platform for building high-performance models with interpretability.
     - Integration with popular data science tools and environments like R, Python, and Hadoop.
   - **Applications**: H2O.ai is used in finance, insurance,

healthcare, and marketing for predictive modeling, risk analysis, and customer insights.

3. **OpenAI**
    - **Overview**: OpenAI is an AI research organization that aims to ensure that artificial general intelligence (AGI) benefits all of humanity. It provides open-source AI tools and models.
    - **Features**:
        - GPT-3: A state-of-the-art language model capable of generating human-like text, used for natural language processing tasks.
        - OpenAI Gym: A toolkit for developing and comparing reinforcement learning algorithms.
        - OpenAI Baselines: High-quality implementations of reinforcement learning algorithms.
    - **Applications**: OpenAI tools are used in research, natural language processing, game development, and automation.

## Applications and Use Cases

1. **Healthcare**
    - **AI Tools**: TensorFlow, PyTorch, Azure AI, and IBM Watson Health.
    - **Use Cases**: Disease diagnosis, personalized treatment plans, drug discovery, medical imaging analysis.
2. **Finance**
    - **AI Tools**: Scikit-learn, H2O.ai, AWS AI, Google Cloud AI.
    - **Use Cases**: Fraud detection, credit scoring, algorithmic trading, customer sentiment analysis.
3. **Retail**
    - **AI Tools**: Keras, Google Cloud AI, Azure AI, Apache Spark.
    - **Use Cases**: Personalized recommendations, inventory management, demand forecasting, customer behavior

analysis.

4. **Manufacturing**
    - **AI Tools**: TensorFlow, AWS AI, H2O.ai, Apache Spark.
    - **Use Cases**: Predictive maintenance, quality control, supply chain optimization, robotics and automation.

5. **Marketing**
    - **AI Tools**: PyTorch, Google Cloud AI, Microsoft Azure AI, H2O.ai.
    - **Use Cases**: Customer segmentation, sentiment analysis, personalized marketing campaigns, lead scoring.

**Conclusion**

The diverse range of AI tools, cloud services, and open-source platforms available today has greatly facilitated the development and deployment of AI applications across various industries. TensorFlow, PyTorch, Keras, and Scikit-learn are some of the popular frameworks that provide robust capabilities for building and training AI models. Cloud AI services from Google, Amazon, and Microsoft offer scalable and flexible solutions for deploying AI at scale. Open-source platforms like Apache Spark, H2O.ai, and OpenAI enable researchers and developers to leverage cutting-edge technologies and contribute to the AI community.

By understanding the features and applications of these AI tools and platforms, businesses and individuals can harness the power of AI to drive innovation, improve efficiency, and create new opportunities. In the following chapters, we will explore case studies of successful AI implementations, strategies for developing and deploying AI responsibly, and the future directions of AI. Through this comprehensive overview, readers can gain a deeper understanding of the AI landscape and its potential impact on various aspects of society.

# CHAPTER 12: CASE STUDIES

## Introduction

Examining real-world applications of Artificial Intelligence (AI) across various industries provides valuable insights into its potential, challenges, and best practices. This chapter presents case studies of successful AI implementations, highlighting the lessons learned from both successes and failures. These case studies span industries such as healthcare, finance, retail, manufacturing, and transportation, showcasing the diverse applications and impacts of AI.

### Case Study 1: Healthcare - IBM Watson for Oncology

1. **Overview**
   - **Organization**: IBM
   - **Application**: IBM Watson for Oncology
   - **Objective**: To leverage AI for personalized cancer treatment recommendations by analyzing patient data and medical literature.
2. **Implementation**
   - **Technology**: IBM Watson uses natural language processing (NLP) and machine learning algorithms to analyze vast amounts of medical data, including clinical guidelines, research papers, and patient records.
   - **Process**: Watson for Oncology processes patient information and suggests evidence-based treatment

options, ranked by confidence levels. Oncologists review these recommendations to make informed decisions.

3. **Successes**

    - **Enhanced Decision-Making**: Watson for Oncology has helped oncologists make more informed treatment decisions by providing comprehensive and up-to-date information.
    - **Improved Patient Outcomes**: Early implementations showed improved patient outcomes due to more personalized and effective treatment plans.

4. **Challenges**

    - **Data Integration**: Integrating diverse datasets from different sources posed significant challenges.
    - **Adoption Resistance**: Some healthcare professionals were initially hesitant to trust AI recommendations over traditional methods.

5. **Lessons Learned**

    - **Data Quality**: High-quality, diverse data is crucial for accurate AI recommendations.
    - **Collaboration**: Collaboration between AI developers and healthcare professionals is essential for successful implementation.
    - **Continuous Improvement**: Regular updates and training are necessary to keep AI systems current with the latest medical research.

## Case Study 2: Finance - JPMorgan Chase COiN

1. **Overview**

    - **Organization**: JPMorgan Chase
    - **Application**: Contract Intelligence (COiN)
    - **Objective**: To automate the review and analysis of legal

documents to improve efficiency and accuracy.
2. **Implementation**
    - **Technology**: COiN uses machine learning and NLP to review complex legal documents and extract critical data points.
    - **Process**: The AI system processes thousands of documents in seconds, identifying relevant information and potential risks.
3. **Successes**
    - **Efficiency Gains**: COiN significantly reduced the time required to review legal documents, from 360,000 hours annually to a matter of seconds.
    - **Cost Savings**: The automation of document review led to substantial cost savings.
4. **Challenges**
    - **Accuracy**: Ensuring the AI system accurately understood and extracted relevant information from diverse legal documents was challenging.
    - **Integration**: Integrating COiN with existing workflows and systems required careful planning and execution.
5. **Lessons Learned**
    - **Thorough Testing**: Extensive testing and validation are crucial to ensure AI accuracy and reliability.
    - **User Training**: Training employees to work effectively with AI systems enhances adoption and utilization.
    - **Scalability**: Designing AI solutions that scale with increasing data volumes and complexity is essential.

## Case Study 3: Retail - Amazon Personalization

1. **Overview**
    - **Organization**: Amazon

- **Application**: Personalized Product Recommendations
- **Objective**: To enhance the customer shopping experience by providing personalized product recommendations.

2. **Implementation**

   - **Technology**: Amazon uses machine learning algorithms to analyze customer behavior, purchase history, and browsing patterns.
   - **Process**: The AI system generates personalized recommendations in real-time, displayed on the website and sent via email.

3. **Successes**

   - **Increased Sales**: Personalized recommendations have significantly boosted sales and customer engagement.
   - **Enhanced Customer Experience**: Customers receive more relevant product suggestions, improving their shopping experience.

4. **Challenges**

   - **Data Privacy**: Ensuring customer data privacy and complying with regulations like GDPR was a key concern.
   - **Algorithm Bias**: Avoiding bias in recommendations to ensure fair and diverse product suggestions.

5. **Lessons Learned**

   - **Ethical Considerations**: Balancing personalization with data privacy and ethical considerations is crucial.
   - **Continuous Optimization**: Regularly updating and optimizing algorithms to reflect changing customer preferences and behavior is necessary.
   - **Transparency**: Providing transparency around data usage and recommendations builds customer trust.

**Case Study 4: Manufacturing - Siemens MindSphere**

# CHAPTER 12: CASE STUDIES | 75

1. **Overview**
   - **Organization**: Siemens
   - **Application**: MindSphere IoT Platform
   - **Objective**: To optimize manufacturing processes through predictive maintenance and real-time data analysis.
2. **Implementation**
   - **Technology**: MindSphere uses AI and IoT to collect and analyze data from industrial machines, predicting maintenance needs and optimizing operations.
   - **Process**: The platform aggregates data from sensors and devices, applying machine learning algorithms to identify patterns and predict failures.
3. **Successes**
   - **Reduced Downtime**: Predictive maintenance has significantly reduced unplanned downtime, improving productivity.
   - **Cost Savings**: Optimized maintenance schedules and reduced equipment failures have led to substantial cost savings.
4. **Challenges**
   - **Data Integration**: Integrating data from diverse industrial machines and sensors posed significant challenges.
   - **Scalability**: Ensuring the platform could scale to handle increasing data volumes and complexity.
5. **Lessons Learned**
   - **Interoperability**: Ensuring interoperability between different machines and systems is essential for successful implementation.
   - **Proactive Maintenance**: Shifting from reactive to

proactive maintenance strategies provides significant benefits.
- **Scalable Architecture**: Designing a scalable architecture that can handle large data volumes and complexity is crucial.

## Case Study 5: Transportation - Uber's AI-Powered Surge Pricing

1. **Overview**
   - **Organization**: Uber
   - **Application**: Surge Pricing Algorithm
   - **Objective**: To balance supply and demand by adjusting prices based on real-time conditions.

2. **Implementation**
   - **Technology**: Uber's surge pricing algorithm uses machine learning to analyze real-time data on rider demand and driver availability.
   - **Process**: The algorithm adjusts fares dynamically based on current conditions, encouraging more drivers to enter high-demand areas.

3. **Successes**
   - **Balanced Supply and Demand**: Surge pricing effectively balances supply and demand, reducing wait times and ensuring availability.
   - **Increased Revenue**: Dynamic pricing has increased revenue for both drivers and Uber.

4. **Challenges**
   - **Customer Perception**: Managing customer perception and dissatisfaction with higher prices during peak times.
   - **Fairness and Transparency**: Ensuring the algorithm is fair and transparent to both drivers and riders.

5. **Lessons Learned**

- **Customer Communication**: Clear communication about how surge pricing works helps manage customer expectations.
- **Fairness**: Ensuring the algorithm is fair and benefits both drivers and riders is crucial for maintaining trust.
- **Transparency**: Providing transparency around pricing decisions builds trust and acceptance.

## Conclusion

These case studies highlight the transformative potential of AI across various industries, showcasing both the successes and challenges encountered during implementation. Key lessons learned include the importance of data quality, collaboration, scalability, transparency, and ethical considerations. By understanding these real-world applications, organizations can better navigate the complexities of AI deployment and leverage its capabilities for innovation and growth.

In the following chapters, we will explore strategies for developing and deploying AI responsibly, ethical considerations, and future directions of AI. By learning from past experiences, readers can better prepare for the opportunities and challenges ahead in this dynamic and rapidly evolving field.

# CHAPTER 13: THE FUTURE OF WORK WITH AI

**Introduction**

Artificial Intelligence (AI) is reshaping the job market, transforming the nature of work, and creating both challenges and opportunities. This chapter discusses the impact of AI on jobs, including job displacement and new opportunities. It also highlights the skills needed for the AI-driven job market and offers insights into how workers and organizations can adapt to this new landscape.

**Impact of AI on Jobs**

1. **Job Displacement**
    - **Overview**: AI and automation are expected to displace certain jobs, particularly those involving repetitive and routine tasks. Industries such as manufacturing, retail, and transportation are likely to experience significant changes.
    - **Examples**:
        - **Manufacturing**: Assembly line workers and machine operators may see their roles replaced by AI-powered robots capable of performing repetitive tasks with high precision.
        - **Retail**: Cashiers and inventory clerks might be

replaced by self-checkout systems and automated inventory management.
    - **Transportation**: Autonomous vehicles could reduce the demand for truck drivers, delivery personnel, and taxi drivers.
2. **Job Transformation**
    - **Overview**: While AI may displace certain jobs, it will also transform existing roles, enhancing productivity and enabling workers to focus on more complex and creative tasks.
    - **Examples**:
        - **Healthcare**: AI assists doctors with diagnostics and treatment planning, allowing them to focus more on patient care and less on administrative tasks.
        - **Finance**: Financial analysts use AI to analyze large datasets, making their roles more strategic and advisory.
        - **Customer Service**: AI chatbots handle routine inquiries, enabling human agents to address more complex customer issues and improve service quality.
3. **Job Creation**
    - **Overview**: AI is expected to create new job opportunities in various sectors, particularly in roles that involve developing, managing, and working alongside AI technologies.
    - **Examples**:
        - **Data Science and Analytics**: The demand for data scientists and analysts is increasing as organizations seek to leverage AI for insights and decision-making.
        - **AI Ethics and Policy**: New roles focused on

ensuring ethical AI use and developing policies for AI governance are emerging.
- **AI Maintenance and Support**: Jobs in maintaining and supporting AI systems, including AI trainers and maintenance technicians, are on the rise.

## New Opportunities in the AI-Driven Job Market

1. **Emerging Job Roles**
   - **AI Specialist**: Professionals who design, develop, and implement AI systems and solutions.
   - **Data Scientist**: Experts in analyzing and interpreting complex data to provide actionable insights and drive decision-making.
   - **Machine Learning Engineer**: Engineers who build and maintain machine learning models and algorithms.
   - **AI Ethics Officer**: Individuals responsible for ensuring that AI systems are developed and used ethically, addressing issues such as bias, fairness, and transparency.
   - **AI Trainer**: Professionals who train AI systems to improve their performance and accuracy by providing labeled data and feedback.

2. **Industry-Specific Opportunities**
   - **Healthcare**: Roles in AI-driven diagnostics, personalized medicine, and health data analysis.
   - **Finance**: Jobs in AI-powered risk assessment, fraud detection, and algorithmic trading.
   - **Retail**: Opportunities in AI-enhanced customer insights, inventory management, and personalized marketing.
   - **Manufacturing**: Positions in AI-based predictive maintenance, quality control, and robotics.

3. **Interdisciplinary Opportunities**

- **AI and Environmental Science**: Roles focused on using AI to address environmental challenges, such as climate modeling and resource management.
- **AI and Education**: Opportunities in developing AI-driven educational tools, personalized learning platforms, and educational data analysis.
- **AI and Creative Industries**: Jobs in AI-assisted content creation, digital art, and music composition.

## Skills Needed for the AI-Driven Job Market

1. **Technical Skills**
   - **Programming Languages**: Proficiency in languages such as Python, R, and Java is essential for developing and implementing AI solutions.
   - **Machine Learning and Deep Learning**: Understanding of machine learning algorithms, neural networks, and deep learning frameworks (e.g., TensorFlow, PyTorch).
   - **Data Science and Analytics**: Skills in data manipulation, statistical analysis, and data visualization tools (e.g., SQL, Tableau).
   - **AI Tools and Platforms**: Familiarity with AI development tools and platforms, such as TensorFlow, PyTorch, and cloud-based AI services.

2. **Analytical and Problem-Solving Skills**
   - **Critical Thinking**: Ability to analyze complex problems, evaluate options, and make data-driven decisions.
   - **Mathematics and Statistics**: Strong foundation in mathematical concepts and statistical methods used in AI and machine learning.
   - **Domain Knowledge**: Understanding of the specific industry or field in which AI is being applied, enabling more effective problem-solving and innovation.

3. **Soft Skills**

- **Communication**: Ability to convey complex technical concepts to non-technical stakeholders and collaborate effectively with diverse teams.
- **Adaptability**: Willingness to learn and adapt to new technologies, methodologies, and changing job requirements.
- **Ethical Awareness**: Understanding of the ethical implications of AI and commitment to developing and using AI responsibly.

4. **Lifelong Learning**

   - **Continuous Education**: Engaging in ongoing education and professional development to stay current with the latest AI advancements and industry trends.
   - **Certifications and Training**: Pursuing certifications and training programs in AI, machine learning, and data science from reputable institutions.

## Adapting to the AI-Driven Job Market

1. **For Workers**

   - **Upskilling and Reskilling**: Investing in education and training to acquire new skills and transition into AI-related roles.
   - **Networking and Collaboration**: Building professional networks and collaborating with peers to share knowledge and stay informed about industry developments.
   - **Embracing Change**: Adopting a proactive mindset towards change and seeking opportunities to innovate and contribute to AI-driven projects.

2. **For Organizations**

   - **Workforce Development**: Implementing training programs and initiatives to upskill and reskill employees for AI-related roles.

- **Ethical AI Practices**: Establishing guidelines and frameworks for the ethical development and use of AI, ensuring fairness, transparency, and accountability.
- **Collaborative Culture**: Fostering a culture of collaboration and continuous learning, encouraging employees to embrace new technologies and methodologies.

3. **For Educational Institutions**
   - **Curriculum Development**: Designing and offering courses and programs focused on AI, machine learning, data science, and related fields.
   - **Industry Partnerships**: Collaborating with industry partners to provide students with hands-on experience and exposure to real-world AI applications.
   - **Lifelong Learning Opportunities**: Offering flexible learning options, such as online courses and certification programs, to support lifelong learning and professional development.

**Conclusion**

The future of work with AI presents both challenges and opportunities. While AI may displace certain jobs, it also creates new roles and transforms existing ones, leading to increased productivity and innovation. To thrive in the AI-driven job market, individuals must acquire the necessary technical, analytical, and soft skills, embrace lifelong learning, and adapt to changing job requirements.

Organizations play a crucial role in supporting their workforce through upskilling and reskilling initiatives, fostering a collaborative culture, and adhering to ethical AI practices. Educational institutions must also evolve to provide relevant and flexible learning opportunities that prepare students for the demands of the AI-driven job market.

By understanding the impact of AI on jobs and the skills

needed for the future, workers, organizations, and educational institutions can better navigate the opportunities and challenges ahead in this dynamic and rapidly evolving field. In the following chapters, we will explore strategies for developing and deploying AI responsibly, ethical considerations, and future directions of AI. Through this comprehensive overview, readers can gain a deeper understanding of the AI landscape and its potential impact on various aspects of society.

# CHAPTER 14: AI RESEARCH AND DEVELOPMENT

## Introduction

Research and development (R&D) in Artificial Intelligence (AI) are critical for pushing the boundaries of what technology can achieve. This chapter explores the leading AI research institutions, current research trends, and the significant role academia plays in advancing AI technology. By understanding these components, we can gain insights into the future directions of AI and its potential to transform various industries and aspects of society.

## Leading AI Research Institutions

1. **OpenAI**
    - **Overview**: Founded with the mission to ensure that artificial general intelligence (AGI) benefits all of humanity, OpenAI conducts cutting-edge research in AI and promotes the responsible use of AI technology.
    - **Notable Projects**:
        - **GPT-3**: A state-of-the-art language model capable of generating human-like text.
        - **DALL-E**: An AI model that creates images from textual descriptions.
    - **Impact**: OpenAI's research has set new benchmarks in natural language processing (NLP) and generative

models, influencing a wide range of applications from chatbots to creative tools.

2. **DeepMind**
   - **Overview**: Acquired by Google in 2015, DeepMind is known for its pioneering work in AI and reinforcement learning.
   - **Notable Projects**:
     - **AlphaGo**: An AI program that defeated the world champion Go player, demonstrating the potential of AI in complex strategic games.
     - **AlphaFold**: An AI system that predicts protein folding with high accuracy, revolutionizing biological research.
   - **Impact**: DeepMind's breakthroughs in reinforcement learning and bioinformatics have significant implications for healthcare, scientific research, and beyond.

3. **MIT Computer Science and Artificial Intelligence Laboratory (CSAIL)**
   - **Overview**: As one of the leading AI research centers, CSAIL focuses on a broad range of AI applications, including robotics, machine learning, and computational biology.
   - **Notable Projects**:
     - **Robust Robotics**: Developing AI algorithms for autonomous navigation in dynamic environments.
     - **AI for Healthcare**: Using AI to improve diagnostics, treatment planning, and patient care.
   - **Impact**: CSAIL's interdisciplinary approach has led to innovations in robotics, healthcare, and AI ethics, influencing both academia and industry.

4. **Stanford Artificial Intelligence Laboratory (SAIL)**
   - **Overview**: Stanford University has been at the

forefront of AI research for decades, with SAIL driving advancements in machine learning, robotics, and AI ethics.
- **Notable Projects**:
  - **ImageNet**: A large visual database designed for use in visual object recognition research.
  - **AI Index**: An annual report tracking global AI progress and trends.
- **Impact**: SAIL's contributions to machine learning, computer vision, and AI policy have shaped the development and deployment of AI technologies worldwide.

5. **Carnegie Mellon University (CMU)**

- **Overview**: CMU's School of Computer Science is renowned for its AI research, particularly in areas such as autonomous systems, NLP, and human-computer interaction.
- **Notable Projects**:
  - **REINFORCE**: Algorithms for reinforcement learning and decision-making.
  - **Linguistic Data Consortium (LDC)**: Resources and tools for language research.
- **Impact**: CMU's research has led to significant advancements in autonomous vehicles, AI-driven language tools, and interactive AI systems.

## Current Research Trends in AI

1. **Reinforcement Learning**

- **Overview**: Reinforcement learning (RL) involves training AI agents to make sequences of decisions by rewarding desired behaviors. RL has seen significant progress, with applications in robotics, gaming, and autonomous systems.
- **Key Developments**:
  - **Deep Q-Networks (DQNs)**: Combining Q-learning

with deep neural networks to play video games at superhuman levels.
- **Policy Optimization Methods**: Techniques like Proximal Policy Optimization (PPO) for more stable and efficient learning.
- **Applications**: RL is used in optimizing logistics, controlling robotic arms, and developing intelligent game agents.

2. **Natural Language Processing (NLP)**
   - **Overview**: NLP focuses on the interaction between computers and human languages. Recent advances in transformer architectures have revolutionized the field.
   - **Key Developments**:
     - **Transformers**: Models like BERT, GPT-3, and T5 that understand and generate human language with high accuracy.
     - **Multilingual Models**: AI systems capable of processing and translating multiple languages.
   - **Applications**: NLP is used in chatbots, translation services, sentiment analysis, and content generation.

3. **Explainable AI (XAI)**
   - **Overview**: Explainable AI aims to make AI decisions more transparent and understandable to humans. This is crucial for trust and accountability in AI systems.
   - **Key Developments**:
     - **Interpretable Models**: Techniques that provide insights into how AI models make decisions, such as LIME (Local Interpretable Model-agnostic Explanations).
     - **Fairness and Bias Detection**: Tools to identify and mitigate bias in AI models.
   - **Applications**: XAI is critical in healthcare, finance, and legal systems where understanding AI decisions is essential.

4. **Federated Learning**

- **Overview**: Federated learning allows AI models to be trained across multiple decentralized devices while keeping data localized. This approach enhances privacy and security.
- **Key Developments**:
  - **Privacy-Preserving Techniques**: Methods like differential privacy and secure multi-party computation.
  - **Scalable Federated Learning**: Algorithms that handle large-scale, distributed data efficiently.
- **Applications**: Federated learning is used in mobile device personalization, healthcare data analysis, and collaborative AI development.

5. **AI for Social Good**

- **Overview**: Research in this area focuses on using AI to address societal challenges, including healthcare, education, and environmental sustainability.
- **Key Developments**:
  - **AI in Disaster Response**: Systems that analyze social media and satellite data to aid in disaster management.
  - **Educational AI**: Tools that provide personalized learning experiences and improve educational outcomes.
- **Applications**: AI for Social Good initiatives aim to enhance public health, promote sustainability, and ensure inclusive education.

## The Role of Academia in Advancing AI Technology

1. **Research and Innovation**

- **Overview**: Academic institutions are at the forefront of AI research, driving innovation through foundational studies and pioneering new methodologies.
- **Key Contributions**:
  - **Theoretical Foundations**: Developing

the mathematical and statistical theories that underpin AI algorithms.
    - **Interdisciplinary Research**: Combining AI with fields like neuroscience, cognitive science, and ethics to broaden its applications and address complex problems.

2. **Education and Workforce Development**
   - **Overview**: Academia plays a crucial role in educating the next generation of AI professionals and researchers.
   - **Key Initiatives**:
     - **AI Curricula**: Offering undergraduate and graduate programs focused on AI, machine learning, and data science.
     - **Workshops and Seminars**: Providing opportunities for continuous learning and professional development through conferences, workshops, and seminars.

3. **Collaboration with Industry**
   - **Overview**: Academic institutions collaborate with industry partners to translate research into practical applications and drive technological advancement.
   - **Key Activities**:
     - **Joint Research Projects**: Partnering with companies to address real-world challenges and develop innovative solutions.
     - **Technology Transfer**: Facilitating the commercialization of academic research through patents, licenses, and startups.

4. **Ethics and Policy Development**
   - **Overview**: Academia contributes to the development of ethical guidelines and policies to ensure the responsible use of AI.
   - **Key Contributions**:
     - **AI Ethics Research**: Investigating the ethical

implications of AI and proposing frameworks for fair and transparent AI systems.
- **Policy Advocacy**: Engaging with policymakers to shape regulations and standards for AI development and deployment.

## Conclusion

AI research and development are driving rapid advancements in technology, with significant contributions from leading research institutions and academia. Current research trends such as reinforcement learning, natural language processing, explainable AI, federated learning, and AI for social good are expanding the capabilities and applications of AI across various domains.

Academia plays a pivotal role in advancing AI technology through research, education, industry collaboration, and policy development. By understanding the landscape of AI research and development, we can better appreciate the potential and challenges of AI, ensuring that its benefits are harnessed responsibly and equitably.

In the following chapters, we will explore practical strategies for developing and deploying AI responsibly, examining case studies of successful AI implementations, and discussing the ethical considerations and future directions of AI. Through this comprehensive overview, readers can gain a deeper understanding of the AI landscape and its potential impact on various aspects of society.

# CHAPTER 15: BUILDING AN AI STRATEGY

**Introduction**

Implementing Artificial Intelligence (AI) in a business can drive innovation, improve efficiency, and create new opportunities for growth. However, developing a successful AI strategy requires careful planning, a clear understanding of objectives, and a roadmap for overcoming challenges. This chapter guides readers on implementing AI in their business, discussing the necessary steps, methods for measuring ROI, and strategies for overcoming adoption challenges.

**Steps to Implementing AI in Business**

1. **Define Objectives and Identify Use Cases**
    - **Overview**: The first step in building an AI strategy is to clearly define the business objectives and identify specific use cases where AI can add value.
    - **Actions**:
        - **Align with Business Goals**: Ensure that AI initiatives align with the overall business strategy and goals.
        - **Identify High-Impact Areas**: Focus on areas where AI can have the most significant impact, such as improving customer experience,

optimizing operations, or enhancing decision-making.
- **Prioritize Use Cases**: Rank potential AI use cases based on factors such as feasibility, potential ROI, and alignment with business priorities.

2. **Assess Data Readiness**
   - **Overview**: Data is the backbone of AI. Assessing data readiness involves evaluating the quality, availability, and completeness of the data required for AI projects.
   - **Actions**:
     - **Data Inventory**: Conduct a data inventory to identify available data sources and assess their quality.
     - **Data Cleaning and Preparation**: Clean and preprocess data to ensure it is suitable for AI models.
     - **Data Governance**: Establish data governance policies to ensure data privacy, security, and compliance with regulations.

3. **Build a Skilled AI Team**
   - **Overview**: Implementing AI requires a team with diverse skills, including data science, machine learning, software engineering, and domain expertise.
   - **Actions**:
     - **Identify Skill Gaps**: Assess the current team's skills and identify gaps that need to be filled.
     - **Hire and Train Talent**: Hire data scientists, machine learning engineers, and other specialists. Provide training and upskilling opportunities for existing employees.
     - **Foster Collaboration**: Encourage collaboration between AI specialists and domain experts to

ensure AI solutions are relevant and effective.

4. **Select the Right Tools and Technologies**
   - **Overview**: Choosing the appropriate AI tools and technologies is crucial for building and deploying AI solutions.
   - **Actions**:
     - **Evaluate AI Platforms**: Assess different AI platforms and tools based on factors such as scalability, ease of use, and integration capabilities.
     - **Leverage Open-Source Tools**: Consider using open-source AI tools and frameworks, which can provide flexibility and cost savings.
     - **Partner with Vendors**: Collaborate with AI vendors and cloud service providers to access advanced AI capabilities and infrastructure.

5. **Develop and Test AI Models**
   - **Overview**: Developing and testing AI models involves iterative experimentation to build models that meet business requirements.
   - **Actions**:
     - **Proof of Concept (PoC)**: Start with a PoC to demonstrate the feasibility and potential value of the AI solution.
     - **Model Development**: Use machine learning and data science techniques to develop AI models. Experiment with different algorithms and feature sets.
     - **Model Validation**: Validate models using real-world data and performance metrics to ensure accuracy and reliability.

6. **Deploy and Scale AI Solutions**

- **Overview**: Once AI models are developed and validated, they need to be deployed and scaled for production use.
- **Actions**:
  - **Deployment Strategy**: Develop a strategy for deploying AI models, including considerations for scalability, performance, and integration with existing systems.
  - **Monitoring and Maintenance**: Implement monitoring to track model performance and retrain models as needed to maintain accuracy.
  - **Iterate and Improve**: Continuously gather feedback and make improvements to AI solutions based on performance data and user feedback.

## Measuring ROI of AI Initiatives

1. **Define Key Performance Indicators (KPIs)**
   - **Overview**: KPIs are metrics that help measure the success and impact of AI initiatives.
   - **Actions**:
     - **Align KPIs with Business Goals**: Ensure KPIs are directly linked to the business objectives of the AI initiative.
     - **Quantitative Metrics**: Use quantitative metrics such as cost savings, revenue growth, time reduction, and accuracy improvements.
     - **Qualitative Metrics**: Include qualitative metrics such as customer satisfaction, employee productivity, and innovation.

2. **Conduct Cost-Benefit Analysis**
   - **Overview**: A cost-benefit analysis helps evaluate the financial viability of AI projects.
   - **Actions**:

- **Identify Costs**: Consider all costs associated with the AI initiative, including technology, infrastructure, training, and ongoing maintenance.
- **Estimate Benefits**: Estimate the potential benefits, including increased revenue, reduced costs, and improved efficiency.
- **Compare Costs and Benefits**: Compare the total costs and benefits to determine the net ROI of the AI initiative.

3. **Track and Report Performance**

   - **Overview**: Regularly tracking and reporting performance helps ensure AI initiatives are on track and delivering expected results.
   - **Actions**:
     - **Performance Dashboards**: Use performance dashboards to visualize and track KPIs and other metrics.
     - **Regular Reviews**: Conduct regular reviews to assess progress and make adjustments as needed.
     - **Stakeholder Communication**: Communicate performance results to stakeholders to ensure transparency and alignment.

## Overcoming AI Adoption Challenges

1. **Addressing Resistance to Change**

   - **Overview**: Resistance to change can hinder AI adoption. Addressing concerns and building a culture of innovation is crucial.
   - **Actions**:
     - **Change Management**: Implement change management strategies to support employees

through the transition.
- **Stakeholder Engagement**: Engage stakeholders early in the process and involve them in decision-making.
- **Education and Training**: Provide education and training to help employees understand AI and its benefits.

2. **Ensuring Data Privacy and Security**
   - **Overview**: Data privacy and security concerns can be a significant barrier to AI adoption.
   - **Actions**:
     - **Data Protection Policies**: Implement robust data protection policies to ensure compliance with regulations such as GDPR and CCPA.
     - **Secure Infrastructure**: Use secure infrastructure and encryption to protect data.
     - **Transparency and Trust**: Be transparent about data usage and build trust with customers and stakeholders.

3. **Managing Ethical and Bias Concerns**
   - **Overview**: Ethical and bias concerns must be addressed to ensure AI solutions are fair and responsible.
   - **Actions**:
     - **Bias Detection and Mitigation**: Implement techniques to detect and mitigate bias in AI models.
     - **Ethical Guidelines**: Develop and follow ethical guidelines for AI development and deployment.
     - **Stakeholder Input**: Involve diverse stakeholders in the development process to ensure different perspectives are considered.

4. **Ensuring Scalability and Integration**
    - **Overview**: Ensuring AI solutions can scale and integrate with existing systems is essential for long-term success.
    - **Actions**:
        - **Scalable Architecture**: Design AI solutions with scalability in mind to handle growing data volumes and user demands.
        - **Integration Strategy**: Develop a strategy for integrating AI solutions with existing systems and workflows.
        - **Continuous Improvement**: Regularly review and improve AI solutions to ensure they remain effective and relevant.

**Conclusion**

Building an AI strategy involves a series of well-defined steps, including defining objectives, assessing data readiness, building a skilled team, selecting the right tools, developing and testing models, and deploying AI solutions. Measuring the ROI of AI initiatives requires defining KPIs, conducting cost-benefit analyses, and tracking performance.

Overcoming adoption challenges involves addressing resistance to change, ensuring data privacy and security, managing ethical and bias concerns, and ensuring scalability and integration. By following these guidelines, businesses can successfully implement AI, drive innovation, and achieve their strategic goals.

In the following chapters, we will explore case studies of successful AI implementations, discuss ethical considerations, and examine future directions of AI. Through this comprehensive overview, readers can gain a deeper understanding of the AI landscape and its potential impact on various aspects of society.

# CHAPTER 16: AI IN EVERYDAY LIFE

**Introduction**

Artificial Intelligence (AI) has seamlessly integrated into various aspects of our daily lives, enhancing convenience, efficiency, and personalization. From personal assistants to social media and smart home devices, AI technologies are transforming how we interact with the world. This chapter showcases how AI is embedded in everyday life, highlighting its impact through practical examples and applications.

**Personal Assistants**

1. **Virtual Assistants**
    - **Overview**: Virtual assistants like Siri, Alexa, and Google Assistant use AI to perform a wide range of tasks, from setting reminders and sending messages to controlling smart home devices.
    - **Features**:
        - **Voice Recognition**: AI-driven voice recognition allows users to interact with their devices using natural language commands.
        - **Task Automation**: Virtual assistants can automate routine tasks, such as scheduling appointments, sending emails, and setting alarms.
        - **Personalization**: These assistants learn user preferences over time, offering personalized recommendations and responses.

- **Applications**:
  - **Daily Management**: Virtual assistants help manage daily activities, from organizing schedules to providing weather updates.
  - **Smart Home Control**: Integration with smart home devices allows users to control lights, thermostats, and security systems with voice commands.
  - **Information Retrieval**: Assistants can quickly retrieve information, answer questions, and provide news updates.

2. **AI in Smartphones**
   - **Overview**: AI enhances smartphone capabilities, making them more intuitive and user-friendly.
   - **Features**:
     - **Camera Enhancements**: AI-powered cameras can automatically adjust settings for optimal photos, recognize scenes, and apply effects.
     - **Battery Management**: AI optimizes battery usage by learning user habits and managing background processes.
     - **Predictive Text and Suggestions**: AI predicts text inputs and provides suggestions, improving typing efficiency and accuracy.
   - **Applications**:
     - **Photography**: AI-driven features like portrait mode, night mode, and real-time editing enhance the quality of smartphone photography.
     - **Security**: Facial recognition and fingerprint scanning use AI to provide secure and convenient access to devices.
     - **Personalized Experience**: AI tailors the user experience by recommending apps, content, and settings based on usage patterns.

**Social Media**

1. **Content Personalization**
   - **Overview**: Social media platforms use AI algorithms to personalize content feeds, ensuring users see relevant posts, ads, and recommendations.
   - **Features**:
     - **Recommendation Systems**: AI analyzes user behavior to recommend posts, videos, and articles that match their interests.
     - **Ad Targeting**: AI targets ads to specific user demographics based on their preferences and browsing history.
     - **Content Filtering**: AI filters and prioritizes content, reducing spam and highlighting trending topics.
   - **Applications**:
     - **News Feeds**: Platforms like Facebook and Twitter use AI to curate personalized news feeds for users.
     - **Video Recommendations**: YouTube's AI suggests videos based on viewing history and engagement.
     - **Advertising**: Businesses use AI-driven ad targeting to reach potential customers more effectively.

2. **User Engagement and Moderation**
   - **Overview**: AI enhances user engagement by fostering interactions and maintaining a safe online environment.
   - **Features**:
     - **Chatbots**: AI-powered chatbots engage with users, answer queries, and provide customer support.
     - **Content Moderation**: AI detects and removes inappropriate content, including hate speech, misinformation, and spam.
     - **Sentiment Analysis**: AI analyzes user comments and feedback to gauge sentiment and improve user experience.

- **Applications**:
  - **Customer Support**: Brands use AI chatbots on social media to provide instant support and resolve issues.
  - **Community Management**: AI helps manage online communities by moderating discussions and enforcing guidelines.
  - **Insights and Analytics**: Social media platforms offer AI-driven analytics tools to help users and businesses understand engagement and trends.

## Home Devices

1. **Smart Home Ecosystems**
   - **Overview**: AI powers smart home devices, creating interconnected ecosystems that enhance convenience, security, and energy efficiency.
   - **Features**:
     - **Voice Control**: AI enables voice control of home devices, allowing users to operate lights, thermostats, and appliances with simple commands.
     - **Automation and Scheduling**: AI automates routine tasks, such as adjusting the thermostat based on occupancy or scheduling lighting changes.
     - **Energy Management**: AI optimizes energy usage by learning user habits and adjusting settings to save energy.
   - **Applications**:
     - **Smart Thermostats**: Devices like Nest use AI to learn user preferences and adjust temperature settings for optimal comfort and efficiency.
     - **Smart Lighting**: AI-powered lighting systems, such as Philips Hue, allow users to control lighting remotely and create schedules.

- **Home Security**: AI enhances home security systems by enabling features like facial recognition, real-time alerts, and automated monitoring.

2. **Home Entertainment**
   - **Overview**: AI improves home entertainment systems by providing personalized content recommendations and enhancing user interactions.
   - **Features**:
     - **Content Recommendations**: AI suggests movies, TV shows, and music based on user preferences and viewing history.
     - **Voice-Activated Controls**: AI-powered voice assistants integrate with entertainment systems, allowing users to search for content and control playback hands-free.
     - **Smart Speakers**: Devices like Amazon Echo and Google Home use AI to play music, answer questions, and control other smart devices.
   - **Applications**:
     - **Streaming Services**: Platforms like Netflix and Spotify use AI to recommend content tailored to individual tastes.
     - **Gaming**: AI enhances gaming experiences through adaptive gameplay, realistic graphics, and personalized recommendations.
     - **Interactive TV**: AI-driven features on smart TVs enable voice search, personalized interfaces, and content suggestions.

## Everyday AI Applications

1. **Healthcare and Fitness**
   - **Overview**: AI-powered healthcare and fitness applications provide personalized insights, track health metrics, and offer virtual assistance.

- **Features**:
  - **Health Monitoring**: Wearable devices with AI track vital signs, activity levels, and sleep patterns.
  - **Virtual Health Assistants**: AI chatbots and apps provide health advice, reminders for medication, and appointment scheduling.
  - **Fitness Coaching**: AI-driven fitness apps offer personalized workout plans, track progress, and provide real-time feedback.
- **Applications**:
  - **Smartwatches**: Devices like Apple Watch and Fitbit use AI to monitor health metrics and provide actionable insights.
  - **Telemedicine**: AI enhances telemedicine platforms by enabling remote diagnostics, virtual consultations, and patient monitoring.
  - **Fitness Apps**: Applications like MyFitnessPal and Nike Training Club use AI to create customized fitness routines and track progress.

2. **Transportation and Navigation**
   - **Overview**: AI enhances transportation and navigation systems by providing real-time traffic updates, optimizing routes, and enabling autonomous driving.
   - **Features**:
     - **Real-Time Traffic Analysis**: AI analyzes traffic data to provide real-time updates and suggest alternate routes.
     - **Autonomous Vehicles**: Self-driving cars use AI to navigate, detect obstacles, and make driving decisions.
     - **Ride-Hailing Services**: AI optimizes ride-hailing services by matching riders with drivers and predicting demand.
   - **Applications**:

- **Navigation Apps**: Apps like Google Maps and Waze use AI to provide accurate navigation and traffic updates.
- **Self-Driving Cars**: Companies like Tesla and Waymo are developing AI-powered autonomous vehicles for safer and more efficient transportation.
- **Ride-Sharing**: Services like Uber and Lyft use AI to improve ride matching, optimize routes, and enhance user experience.

3. **Shopping and Retail**
   - **Overview**: AI transforms shopping and retail experiences by offering personalized recommendations, automating customer service, and enhancing inventory management.
   - **Features**:
     - **Personalized Recommendations**: AI analyzes user behavior to recommend products and services tailored to individual preferences.
     - **Automated Customer Service**: AI chatbots assist customers with inquiries, process orders, and provide support.
     - **Inventory Optimization**: AI helps retailers manage inventory levels, predict demand, and reduce stockouts.
   - **Applications**:
     - **E-Commerce Platforms**: Websites like Amazon and eBay use AI to recommend products and personalize the shopping experience.
     - **Virtual Shopping Assistants**: AI-powered assistants help customers find products, compare prices, and make purchases.
     - **Smart Stores**: Retailers like Walmart and Alibaba use AI to optimize store layouts, manage inventory, and enhance customer service.

## Conclusion

AI has become an integral part of everyday life, enhancing convenience, personalization, and efficiency across various domains. From personal assistants and social media to smart home devices and beyond, AI technologies are transforming how we interact with the world. By understanding the diverse applications of AI in everyday life, we can better appreciate its impact and potential for future innovations.

In the following chapters, we will explore strategies for developing and deploying AI responsibly, discuss ethical considerations, and examine future directions of AI. Through this comprehensive overview, readers can gain a deeper understanding of the AI landscape and its potential impact on various aspects of society.

# CHAPTER 17: AI AND CYBERSECURITY

**Introduction**

As the digital landscape expands, so do the threats to cybersecurity. Traditional security measures are increasingly inadequate against sophisticated cyber attacks. Artificial Intelligence (AI) is revolutionizing cybersecurity by enhancing threat detection, response, and prevention capabilities. This chapter explores the role of AI in cybersecurity, including its applications in threat detection and response, and highlights the challenges associated with AI-based security systems.

**The Role of AI in Enhancing Cybersecurity**

1. **AI-Driven Threat Detection**
    - **Overview**: AI improves threat detection by analyzing vast amounts of data to identify patterns and anomalies indicative of cyber threats.
    - **Features**:
        - **Anomaly Detection**: AI systems can detect unusual patterns of behavior that may signify a security breach, such as unusual login times or data access patterns.
        - **Signature-Based Detection**: AI can rapidly analyze and compare signatures of known malware to identify threats.
        - **Behavioral Analysis**: AI models analyze the

behavior of users and systems to detect deviations from normal activity, which might indicate malicious intent.
- **Applications**:
  - **Intrusion Detection Systems (IDS)**: AI-powered IDS can identify unauthorized access and unusual activities in real-time.
  - **Endpoint Protection**: AI enhances endpoint security by detecting and responding to threats on individual devices.

2. **AI-Enhanced Incident Response**
   - **Overview**: AI automates and accelerates the incident response process, reducing the time between threat detection and mitigation.
   - **Features**:
     - **Automated Responses**: AI systems can automatically isolate affected systems, terminate malicious processes, and remove malware.
     - **Threat Intelligence Integration**: AI integrates with threat intelligence platforms to provide real-time updates and contextual information about emerging threats.
     - **Forensic Analysis**: AI tools assist in forensic investigations by analyzing attack patterns and identifying the root cause of incidents.
   - **Applications**:
     - **Security Information and Event Management (SIEM)**: AI-powered SIEM systems analyze security alerts in real-time, prioritize incidents, and automate responses.
     - **Incident Response Platforms**: AI-driven platforms streamline incident response workflows, ensuring quick and effective action

against cyber threats.

3. **Predictive Threat Analysis**
   - **Overview**: AI predicts potential threats by analyzing historical data and identifying patterns that precede cyber attacks.
   - **Features**:
     - **Machine Learning Models**: AI uses machine learning algorithms to predict the likelihood of future attacks based on past incidents and threat intelligence.
     - **Risk Scoring**: AI assigns risk scores to assets and activities, enabling proactive measures to mitigate high-risk vulnerabilities.
     - **Proactive Defense**: AI enables organizations to anticipate attacks and implement preventive measures before threats materialize.
   - **Applications**:
     - **Vulnerability Management**: AI identifies and prioritizes vulnerabilities that are most likely to be exploited, allowing for timely patching and mitigation.
     - **Threat Hunting**: AI assists security teams in proactively searching for threats within the network before they can cause harm.

## Challenges of AI-Based Security Systems

1. **Data Quality and Availability**
   - **Overview**: The effectiveness of AI in cybersecurity heavily depends on the quality and availability of data used for training models.
   - **Challenges**:
     - **Incomplete Data**: Incomplete or inaccurate data can lead to false positives and false negatives in

threat detection.
- **Data Privacy**: Collecting and analyzing large volumes of data can raise privacy concerns and regulatory compliance issues.
- **Data Silos**: Security data is often scattered across different systems and formats, making it challenging to aggregate and analyze comprehensively.
- **Solutions**:
  - **Data Normalization**: Implement data normalization techniques to ensure consistency and completeness.
  - **Data Anonymization**: Use anonymization techniques to protect sensitive information while still enabling effective analysis.
  - **Centralized Data Repositories**: Establish centralized repositories for security data to facilitate comprehensive analysis.

2. **Evolving Threat Landscape**
   - **Overview**: Cyber threats are constantly evolving, and AI models must adapt to new attack vectors and tactics.
   - **Challenges**:
     - **Adversarial Attacks**: Attackers may use adversarial techniques to deceive AI models, causing them to misclassify or overlook threats.
     - **Rapidly Changing Tactics**: Cybercriminals frequently update their tactics, techniques, and procedures (TTPs), requiring continuous model updates.
     - **Zero-Day Exploits**: New, previously unknown vulnerabilities (zero-day exploits) can bypass traditional AI-based defenses.
   - **Solutions**:

- **Continuous Learning**: Implement continuous learning and model retraining to keep up with the evolving threat landscape.
- **Adversarial Training**: Use adversarial training techniques to improve the robustness of AI models against deceptive attacks.
- **Threat Intelligence Sharing**: Participate in threat intelligence sharing communities to stay informed about emerging threats and vulnerabilities.

3. **Integration with Existing Systems**
   - **Overview**: Integrating AI solutions with existing cybersecurity infrastructure can be complex and resource-intensive.
   - **Challenges**:
     - **Compatibility Issues**: Ensuring compatibility between AI tools and existing security systems can be challenging.
     - **Scalability**: AI solutions must be scalable to handle increasing data volumes and more complex threat environments.
     - **Resource Allocation**: Implementing AI requires significant investment in hardware, software, and skilled personnel.
   - **Solutions**:
     - **Modular Integration**: Use modular AI solutions that can be integrated incrementally with existing systems.
     - **Cloud-Based AI Services**: Leverage cloud-based AI services to scale resources as needed without significant upfront investment.
     - **Cross-Functional Teams**: Establish cross-functional teams to oversee the integration

process and ensure seamless operation.

4. **Ethical and Legal Concerns**

- **Overview**: The use of AI in cybersecurity raises ethical and legal concerns, particularly regarding data privacy and decision-making transparency.
- **Challenges**:
  - **Bias in AI Models**: AI models may inadvertently incorporate biases, leading to unfair or discriminatory outcomes.
  - **Transparency and Accountability**: Ensuring transparency in AI decision-making processes is critical for accountability and trust.
  - **Regulatory Compliance**: Adhering to data protection regulations and standards is essential to avoid legal repercussions.
- **Solutions**:
  - **Fairness Audits**: Conduct regular fairness audits to identify and mitigate biases in AI models.
  - **Explainable AI (XAI)**: Develop explainable AI models that provide clear and understandable reasoning for their decisions.
  - **Compliance Frameworks**: Implement compliance frameworks to ensure adherence to relevant data protection regulations and standards.

## Conclusion

AI is transforming cybersecurity by enhancing threat detection, response, and prevention capabilities. AI-driven solutions offer significant advantages, including real-time threat analysis, automated incident response, and predictive threat analysis. However, challenges such as data quality, evolving threats, integration complexity, and ethical concerns must be addressed to maximize the effectiveness of AI in cybersecurity.

By understanding the role of AI in cybersecurity and addressing these challenges, organizations can better protect their digital assets and stay ahead of cyber threats. In the following chapters, we will explore case studies of successful AI implementations, discuss strategies for developing and deploying AI responsibly, and examine future directions of AI. Through this comprehensive overview, readers can gain a deeper understanding of the AI landscape and its potential impact on various aspects of society.

# CHAPTER 18: INTERDISCIPLINARY APPROACHES TO AI

**Introduction**

Artificial Intelligence (AI) is not confined to traditional fields such as computer science and engineering. It intersects with various other disciplines, enhancing creativity, driving scientific research, and transforming the arts. This chapter explores how AI intersects with fields like art, creativity, and scientific research, highlighting interdisciplinary AI applications and their potential impacts.

**AI in Art and Creativity**

1. **Generative Art**
   - **Overview**: AI can create new forms of art by generating images, music, and even literature, pushing the boundaries of creativity and expanding artistic possibilities.
   - **Features**:
     - **Neural Networks**: AI algorithms, particularly generative adversarial networks (GANs), create realistic images and artworks.
     - **Music Composition**: AI models like OpenAI's MuseNet and Google's Magenta generate original music compositions in various styles.

- **Literature and Poetry**: AI tools such as GPT-3 can write poems, stories, and articles, mimicking human creativity.
- **Applications**:
  - **Visual Arts**: AI-generated artworks have been showcased in galleries and sold at auctions, exemplifying the integration of AI in visual arts.
  - **Music Production**: Musicians and composers use AI tools to create new melodies, harmonize tracks, and experiment with innovative sounds.
  - **Creative Writing**: Authors and content creators use AI to generate ideas, write drafts, and enhance their creative output.

2. **Interactive Art Installations**

   - **Overview**: AI-powered interactive installations create immersive experiences by responding to viewers' actions and emotions.
   - **Features**:
     - **Computer Vision**: AI uses computer vision to interpret and respond to viewers' movements and gestures.
     - **Natural Language Processing (NLP)**: AI systems understand and respond to verbal inputs, creating dynamic interactions.
     - **Emotion Recognition**: AI detects and reacts to viewers' emotional expressions, making the installations more engaging.
   - **Applications**:
     - **Museums and Galleries**: AI-driven installations in museums and galleries offer interactive and personalized experiences for visitors.
     - **Public Spaces**: Interactive art in public

spaces engages communities and encourages participation.
- **Performance Art**: Artists integrate AI into performances, creating real-time, adaptive shows that respond to audience feedback.

3. **Collaborative Creativity**
    - **Overview**: AI serves as a collaborative partner for artists, helping them explore new ideas and techniques.
    - **Features**:
        - **Idea Generation**: AI generates new concepts and suggests creative directions.
        - **Design Assistance**: AI tools assist in designing and prototyping, speeding up the creative process.
        - **Customization**: AI enables personalized art experiences, tailoring creations to individual preferences.
    - **Applications**:
        - **Fashion Design**: Designers use AI to explore innovative patterns, materials, and styles.
        - **Graphic Design**: AI tools like Adobe Sensei assist graphic designers by automating repetitive tasks and suggesting creative enhancements.
        - **Film and Animation**: AI helps in storyboarding, visual effects, and character creation, enhancing the creative workflow.

## AI in Scientific Research

1. **Data Analysis and Discovery**
    - **Overview**: AI accelerates scientific discovery by analyzing large datasets, identifying patterns, and generating insights.
    - **Features**:

- **Machine Learning Models**: AI algorithms analyze complex datasets, finding correlations and making predictions.
- **Data Mining**: AI extracts valuable information from vast amounts of unstructured data, facilitating research.
- **Simulation and Modeling**: AI enhances the accuracy and efficiency of simulations and models used in scientific research.
  - **Applications**:
    - **Genomics**: AI analyzes genetic data to identify disease markers and understand genetic variations.
    - **Astronomy**: AI processes astronomical data to discover new celestial objects and phenomena.
    - **Climate Science**: AI models predict climate patterns and analyze environmental data to study climate change.

2. **Drug Discovery and Development**
   - **Overview**: AI transforms the pharmaceutical industry by speeding up the drug discovery and development process.
   - **Features**:
     - **Predictive Modeling**: AI predicts how different compounds will interact with biological targets, reducing the need for extensive laboratory testing.
     - **Molecular Simulation**: AI simulates molecular structures and interactions, aiding in the design of new drugs.
     - **Clinical Trials Optimization**: AI identifies suitable candidates for clinical trials and predicts trial outcomes.

- **Applications**:
  - **Target Identification**: AI helps identify new drug targets by analyzing biological data and disease mechanisms.
  - **Lead Optimization**: AI refines potential drug candidates, optimizing their efficacy and safety profiles.
  - **Personalized Medicine**: AI tailors treatments to individual patients based on their genetic profiles and medical histories.

3. **Environmental Science**
   - **Overview**: AI addresses environmental challenges by providing tools for monitoring, predicting, and mitigating environmental issues.
   - **Features**:
     - **Remote Sensing**: AI processes satellite imagery and remote sensing data to monitor environmental changes.
     - **Predictive Analytics**: AI models predict environmental events such as natural disasters, helping in disaster preparedness and response.
     - **Sustainability Solutions**: AI identifies sustainable practices and optimizes resource management.
   - **Applications**:
     - **Wildlife Conservation**: AI tracks animal populations and detects illegal activities like poaching.
     - **Agriculture**: AI enhances precision farming techniques, improving crop yields and reducing environmental impact.
     - **Climate Modeling**: AI improves the accuracy of climate models, helping scientists understand and

address climate change.

**Interdisciplinary AI Applications**

1. **AI in Healthcare**
   - **Overview**: AI intersects with healthcare to improve diagnostics, treatment, and patient care.
   - **Applications**:
     - **Medical Imaging**: AI analyzes medical images to detect diseases such as cancer, enabling early diagnosis and treatment.
     - **Telemedicine**: AI-powered platforms facilitate remote consultations and personalized healthcare.
     - **Predictive Healthcare**: AI predicts disease outbreaks and patient outcomes, aiding in preventive care.

2. **AI in Education**
   - **Overview**: AI enhances education by providing personalized learning experiences and automating administrative tasks.
   - **Applications**:
     - **Adaptive Learning**: AI tailors educational content to individual learning styles and paces.
     - **Automated Grading**: AI automates the grading process, providing instant feedback to students.
     - **Virtual Tutors**: AI-driven virtual tutors assist students with their studies, offering personalized support.

3. **AI in Business and Industry**
   - **Overview**: AI optimizes business operations, enhances decision-making, and drives innovation across various industries.

- **Applications**:
  - **Customer Service**: AI chatbots handle customer inquiries and provide support, improving customer satisfaction.
  - **Supply Chain Management**: AI optimizes supply chain operations, reducing costs and improving efficiency.
  - **Financial Analysis**: AI analyzes financial data to predict market trends and make investment recommendations.

4. **AI in Public Safety and Law Enforcement**
   - **Overview**: AI supports public safety and law enforcement efforts by enhancing surveillance, crime detection, and resource allocation.
   - **Applications**:
     - **Surveillance Systems**: AI-powered surveillance systems monitor public spaces and detect suspicious activities.
     - **Predictive Policing**: AI analyzes crime data to predict and prevent criminal activities.
     - **Resource Management**: AI optimizes the allocation of law enforcement resources, improving response times and effectiveness.

**Conclusion**

AI's interdisciplinary applications demonstrate its transformative potential across various fields, from art and creativity to scientific research and beyond. By integrating AI with different disciplines, we can unlock new possibilities, drive innovation, and address complex challenges. Understanding these interdisciplinary approaches helps us appreciate the broader impact of AI and its potential to enhance various aspects of society.

In the following chapters, we will explore practical strategies for developing and deploying AI responsibly, discuss ethical considerations, and examine future directions of AI. Through this comprehensive overview, readers can gain a deeper understanding of the AI landscape and its potential impact on various aspects of society.

# CHAPTER 19: EDUCATIONAL RESOURCES FOR AI

**Introduction**

As the field of Artificial Intelligence (AI) continues to evolve, staying informed and continually learning is essential for anyone interested in this domain. This chapter provides a comprehensive list of resources for learning about AI, including online courses, books, journals, conferences, and workshops. These resources cater to a range of expertise levels, from beginners to advanced practitioners, and cover various aspects of AI, including machine learning, deep learning, natural language processing, and AI ethics.

**Online Courses**

1. **Coursera**
   - **Machine Learning by Stanford University**
     - **Instructor**: Andrew Ng
     - **Overview**: This course provides a broad introduction to machine learning, data mining, and statistical pattern recognition.
     - **Topics Covered**: Supervised learning, unsupervised learning, best practices in machine learning.
   - **Deep Learning Specialization**

- **Instructor**: Andrew Ng and deeplearning.ai team
- **Overview**: A comprehensive course series covering deep learning fundamentals, including neural networks, convolutional networks, and sequence models.

2. **edX**
    - **AI for Everyone by IBM**
        - **Overview**: Designed for non-technical learners, this course explains AI concepts and business applications.
        - **Topics Covered**: AI terminology, machine learning, AI applications in business.
    - **MicroMasters Program in Artificial Intelligence by Columbia University**
        - **Overview**: A series of graduate-level courses that provide a deep understanding of AI.
        - **Topics Covered**: Machine learning, robotics, computer animation.

3. **Udacity**
    - **Artificial Intelligence Nanodegree**
        - **Overview**: An in-depth program designed to teach AI principles and practices.
        - **Topics Covered**: Search and optimization, logic and reasoning, probabilistic models, machine learning.
    - **Deep Reinforcement Learning Nanodegree**
        - **Overview**: Focuses on the application of deep learning and reinforcement learning techniques.
        - **Topics Covered**: Value-based methods, policy-based methods, multi-agent reinforcement learning.

4. **Khan Academy**

- Introduction to Algorithms and Machine Learning
  - **Overview**: A beginner-friendly course covering the basics of algorithms and machine learning.
  - **Topics Covered**: Algorithm design, sorting algorithms, machine learning principles.

**Books**

1. **"Artificial Intelligence: A Modern Approach" by Stuart Russell and Peter Norvig**
   - **Overview**: A comprehensive textbook widely used in AI courses.
   - **Topics Covered**: Search algorithms, knowledge representation, planning, machine learning, and robotics.

2. **"Deep Learning" by Ian Goodfellow, Yoshua Bengio, and Aaron Courville**
   - **Overview**: A detailed guide to deep learning theory and practice.
   - **Topics Covered**: Neural networks, optimization algorithms, convolutional networks, sequence modeling.

3. **"Hands-On Machine Learning with Scikit-Learn, Keras, and TensorFlow" by Aurélien Géron**
   - **Overview**: A practical guide to machine learning using Python libraries.
   - **Topics Covered**: Data preprocessing, regression, classification, neural networks, deep learning.

4. **"Pattern Recognition and Machine Learning" by Christopher M. Bishop**
   - **Overview**: A foundational book on machine learning and pattern recognition.
   - **Topics Covered**: Bayesian networks, graphical models,

mixture models, sequential data.

5. **"Superintelligence: Paths, Dangers, Strategies" by Nick Bostrom**
   - **Overview**: An exploration of the potential risks and benefits of developing superintelligent AI.
   - **Topics Covered**: Future of AI, ethical considerations, strategic implications.

**Journals**

1. **Journal of Artificial Intelligence Research (JAIR)**
   - **Overview**: Publishes high-quality research articles on all aspects of AI.
   - **Topics Covered**: Theoretical AI, applications, machine learning, natural language processing.
2. **Artificial Intelligence Journal (AIJ)**
   - **Overview**: Focuses on the publication of original research in all areas of AI.
   - **Topics Covered**: Cognitive modeling, knowledge representation, reasoning, learning.
3. **Machine Learning Journal**
   - **Overview**: Covers research on all aspects of machine learning.
   - **Topics Covered**: Supervised learning, unsupervised learning, reinforcement learning, applications.
4. **IEEE Transactions on Neural Networks and Learning Systems**
   - **Overview**: Publishes technical papers on neural networks and learning systems.
   - **Topics Covered**: Neural network architectures, learning algorithms, applications.
5. **AI Magazine**

- **Overview**: Aims to publish informative articles on AI research, applications, and education.
- **Topics Covered**: Current AI research, innovative applications, AI education.

## Conferences

1. **Neural Information Processing Systems (NeurIPS)**
   - **Overview**: A leading conference in AI and machine learning.
   - **Topics Covered**: Neural networks, deep learning, reinforcement learning, AI applications.
2. **International Conference on Machine Learning (ICML)**
   - **Overview**: One of the premier conferences on machine learning.
   - **Topics Covered**: Theoretical machine learning, applied machine learning, algorithm development.
3. **Conference on Computer Vision and Pattern Recognition (CVPR)**
   - **Overview**: Focuses on computer vision and pattern recognition research.
   - **Topics Covered**: Image processing, object detection, video analysis, deep learning in computer vision.
4. **Association for the Advancement of Artificial Intelligence (AAAI) Conference**
   - **Overview**: A major AI conference covering a broad range of AI topics.
   - **Topics Covered**: Knowledge representation, reasoning, machine learning, AI ethics.
5. **International Joint Conference on Artificial Intelligence (IJCAI)**
   - **Overview**: Brings together researchers from around the

world to discuss advancements in AI.
- **Topics Covered**: AI theory, applications, interdisciplinary AI research.

**Workshops and Seminars**

1. **AI for Good Global Summit**
   - **Overview**: Focuses on using AI to address global challenges.
   - **Topics Covered**: AI for sustainable development, ethics in AI, AI applications in health and education.

2. **Machine Learning Summer Schools (MLSS)**
   - **Overview**: Intensive courses on machine learning and AI for students and professionals.
   - **Topics Covered**: Fundamentals of machine learning, advanced topics, practical applications.

3. **Deep Learning Indaba**
   - **Overview**: Aims to strengthen AI and machine learning in Africa through teaching and networking.
   - **Topics Covered**: Deep learning techniques, research presentations, collaborative projects.

4. **Stanford AI4ALL**
   - **Overview**: A summer program for high school students to learn about AI and its societal impact.
   - **Topics Covered**: AI fundamentals, ethics in AI, hands-on projects.

5. **Re·Work Deep Learning Summit**
   - **Overview**: Brings together industry leaders and researchers to discuss deep learning innovations.
   - **Topics Covered**: Latest deep learning research, AI applications, industry trends.

**Conclusion**

A wealth of educational resources is available for learning about AI, catering to various levels of expertise and interests. Online courses, books, journals, conferences, and workshops provide valuable knowledge and insights into AI principles, practices, and applications. By leveraging these resources, learners can stay informed about the latest developments in AI, enhance their skills, and contribute to the advancement of this dynamic field.

In the following chapters, we will explore case studies of successful AI implementations, discuss strategies for developing and deploying AI responsibly, and examine future directions of AI. Through this comprehensive overview, readers can gain a deeper understanding of the AI landscape and its potential impact on various aspects of society.

# CHAPTER 20: CONCLUSION

**Introduction**

Artificial Intelligence (AI) has emerged as a transformative technology, reshaping industries, driving innovation, and influencing our daily lives. This chapter summarizes the impact of AI, provides an outlook on its future, and offers final thoughts on the importance of staying informed about AI trends.

**Summary of AI's Impact**

1. **Transforming Industries**

    - **Healthcare**: AI is revolutionizing healthcare by enabling early disease detection, personalized treatment plans, and efficient administrative processes. AI-driven diagnostic tools, such as image recognition for radiology, and predictive analytics for patient outcomes, are enhancing the quality of care.
    - **Finance**: AI enhances financial services through fraud detection, risk management, and automated trading. Machine learning algorithms analyze vast datasets to identify patterns, predict market trends, and make data-driven decisions, increasing efficiency and accuracy in financial operations.
    - **Retail**: AI optimizes retail operations by improving inventory management, personalizing customer experiences, and automating customer

service. Recommendation systems, dynamic pricing, and chatbots are some examples of how AI is enhancing the retail sector.

- **Manufacturing**: AI-driven automation, predictive maintenance, and quality control are transforming manufacturing processes. Robotics and AI enable manufacturers to increase productivity, reduce downtime, and maintain high-quality standards.
- **Transportation**: AI is pivotal in the development of autonomous vehicles, optimizing logistics, and enhancing traffic management. Self-driving cars, AI-powered route optimization, and intelligent traffic systems are making transportation safer and more efficient.

2. **Enhancing Daily Life**

- **Personal Assistants**: AI-powered virtual assistants like Siri, Alexa, and Google Assistant streamline daily tasks, from setting reminders and sending messages to controlling smart home devices.
- **Smart Home Devices**: AI integrates with home devices to create connected, efficient, and user-friendly living environments. Smart thermostats, lighting systems, and security cameras are examples of AI's influence in homes.
- **Social Media**: AI personalizes content feeds, improves user engagement, and enhances content moderation on social media platforms. Algorithms analyze user behavior to deliver relevant content and maintain a safe online environment.

3. **Driving Scientific Research**

- **Drug Discovery**: AI accelerates drug discovery and development by predicting molecular interactions, optimizing clinical trials, and identifying potential treatments. AI models analyze biological data to

identify promising drug candidates and streamline the development process.
- **Environmental Science**: AI aids in environmental monitoring, climate modeling, and conservation efforts. Remote sensing, predictive analytics, and AI-driven simulations help scientists address environmental challenges and promote sustainability.
- **Astronomy**: AI processes astronomical data to discover new celestial objects, analyze cosmic phenomena, and predict space weather. Machine learning algorithms assist astronomers in identifying patterns and making significant discoveries.

4. **Interdisciplinary Applications**
   - **Art and Creativity**: AI enhances artistic creativity through generative art, interactive installations, and collaborative tools. AI algorithms create new forms of art, assist in design processes, and offer personalized artistic experiences.
   - **Education**: AI personalizes learning experiences, automates administrative tasks, and provides virtual tutoring. Adaptive learning platforms, automated grading systems, and AI-driven educational tools improve teaching and learning outcomes.
   - **Public Safety**: AI supports public safety and law enforcement by enhancing surveillance, predictive policing, and resource management. AI-driven systems monitor public spaces, analyze crime data, and optimize the allocation of resources.

## Outlook on the Future of AI

1. **Advancements in AI Technology**
   - **Quantum Computing**: Quantum computing holds the potential to revolutionize AI by solving complex problems faster than classical computers. Quantum AI

could enhance machine learning algorithms, optimize simulations, and drive significant advancements in various fields.

- **Explainable AI (XAI)**: As AI systems become more complex, the need for transparency and interpretability increases. XAI aims to make AI decision-making processes understandable, enhancing trust and accountability.
- **Federated Learning**: Federated learning enables AI models to be trained across decentralized devices while maintaining data privacy. This approach enhances data security and allows for collaborative AI development without compromising sensitive information.

2. **Ethical and Responsible AI**

- **Bias and Fairness**: Addressing bias in AI models is crucial for ensuring fairness and equity. Developing techniques to detect and mitigate bias, promoting diversity in training data, and establishing ethical guidelines are essential steps.
- **Privacy and Security**: Ensuring data privacy and security in AI applications is critical. Implementing robust data protection measures, adhering to regulations, and fostering transparency are vital for maintaining user trust.
- **Regulation and Governance**: Establishing regulatory frameworks and governance structures is necessary for the responsible development and deployment of AI. Collaboration between governments, industry, and academia is essential for creating effective policies and standards.

3. **Integration with Emerging Technologies**

- **Internet of Things (IoT)**: The integration of AI with IoT enhances the capabilities of connected devices, enabling smarter and more responsive systems. AI-driven IoT applications include smart cities, industrial automation, and healthcare monitoring.

- **Blockchain**: Combining AI with blockchain technology can enhance data security, transparency, and traceability. Applications include secure data sharing, decentralized AI models, and fraud detection.
- **Augmented Reality (AR) and Virtual Reality (VR)**: AI enhances AR and VR experiences by providing realistic simulations, intelligent interactions, and personalized content. Applications range from gaming and entertainment to training and education.

**Final Thoughts and Reflections**

1. **Staying Informed about AI Trends**

    - **Continuous Learning**: The rapid evolution of AI necessitates continuous learning and staying updated with the latest advancements. Engaging with educational resources, attending conferences, and participating in workshops are essential for maintaining knowledge and skills.
    - **Collaborative Efforts**: Collaboration between researchers, practitioners, policymakers, and educators is crucial for advancing AI responsibly. Sharing knowledge, best practices, and ethical considerations helps in addressing challenges and maximizing the benefits of AI.
    - **Ethical Considerations**: Emphasizing ethical considerations in AI development and deployment ensures that AI technologies are used for the greater good. Fostering a culture of responsibility and accountability is essential for building trust and promoting the positive impact of AI.

2. **The Transformative Potential of AI**

    - **Innovation and Efficiency**: AI drives innovation

and efficiency across various sectors, creating new opportunities and improving existing processes. Embracing AI's potential can lead to significant advancements and positive outcomes.

- **Empowering Individuals**: AI empowers individuals by enhancing capabilities, providing personalized experiences, and improving quality of life. From healthcare and education to daily convenience, AI's influence is profound and far-reaching.
- **Addressing Global Challenges**: AI has the potential to address some of the most pressing global challenges, including healthcare, climate change, and resource management. Leveraging AI for social good can lead to sustainable and equitable solutions.

**Conclusion**

Artificial Intelligence is a transformative force that is reshaping industries, enhancing daily life, and driving scientific research. Its interdisciplinary applications and integration with emerging technologies highlight its vast potential and impact. As AI continues to evolve, staying informed about its trends, advancements, and ethical considerations is essential for harnessing its benefits responsibly.

By embracing continuous learning, fostering collaboration, and prioritizing ethical considerations, we can navigate the challenges and opportunities presented by AI. The future of AI holds immense promise, and its responsible development and deployment will shape a better and more innovative world.

# CITATION LIST

**Chapter 1: Introduction to Artificial Intelligence and Technology Trends**

1. Turing, A. M. (1950). Computing Machinery and Intelligence. Mind, 59(236), 433-460.
2. Russell, S., & Norvig, P. (2020). Artificial Intelligence: A Modern Approach. 4th ed. Pearson.

**Chapter 2: Historical Development of Artificial Intelligence** 3. McCarthy, J., Minsky, M. L., Rochester, N., & Shannon, C. E. (1956). A Proposal for the Dartmouth Summer Research Project on Artificial Intelligence. 4. Newell, A., & Simon, H. A. (1956). The Logic Theory Machine. IRE Transactions on Information Theory, 2(3), 61-79.

**Chapter 3: Core Concepts of Artificial Intelligence** 5. Goodfellow, I., Bengio, Y., & Courville, A. (2016). Deep Learning. MIT Press. 6. Murphy, K. P. (2012). Machine Learning: A Probabilistic Perspective. MIT Press.

**Chapter 4: Current Trends in Artificial Intelligence** 7. Chui, M., Manyika, J., & Miremadi, M. (2018). What AI Can and Can't Do (Yet) for Your Business. McKinsey Quarterly. 8. Topol, E. (2019). Deep Medicine: How Artificial Intelligence Can Make Healthcare Human Again. Basic Books.

**Chapter 5: AI and the Internet of Things (IoT)** 9. Lee, I., & Lee, K. (2015). The Internet of Things (IoT): Applications, investments, and challenges for enterprises. Business Horizons, 58(4), 431-440. 10. Minerva, R., Biru, A., & Rotondi, D. (2015). Towards a Definition of the Internet of Things (IoT). IEEE Internet Initiative.

**Chapter 6: Big Data and AI** 11. Marr, B. (2018). Big Data in Practice: How 45 Successful Companies Used Big Data Analytics to Deliver Extraordinary Results. Wiley. 12. Provost, F., & Fawcett, T. (2013). Data Science for Business: What You Need to Know about Data Mining and Data-Analytic Thinking. O'Reilly Media.

**Chapter 7: AI in Business and Industry** 13. Davenport, T. H., & Kirby, J. (2016). Just How Smart Are Smart Machines? Sloan Management Review. 14. Barlow, M. (2016). Real-World AI: A Practical Guide for Responsible Machine Learning. O'Reilly Media.

**Chapter 8: AI and Automation** 15. Brynjolfsson, E., & McAfee, A. (2014). The Second Machine Age: Work, Progress, and Prosperity in a Time of Brilliant Technologies. W.W. Norton & Company. 16. Ford, M. (2015). Rise of the Robots: Technology and the Threat of a Jobless Future. Basic Books.

**Chapter 9: Ethics and AI** 17. O'Neil, C. (2016). Weapons of Math Destruction: How Big Data Increases Inequality and Threatens Democracy. Crown Publishing Group. 18. Bostrom, N., & Yudkowsky, E. (2014). The Ethics of Artificial Intelligence. In The Cambridge Handbook of Artificial Intelligence, Cambridge University Press.

**Chapter 10: Future Trends in AI** 19. Kelly, K. (2016). The Inevitable: Understanding the 12 Technological Forces That Will Shape Our Future. Viking. 20. Tegmark, M. (2017). Life 3.0: Being Human in the Age of Artificial Intelligence. Knopf.

**Chapter 11: AI Tools and Platforms** 21. Géron, A. (2019). Hands-On Machine Learning with Scikit-Learn, Keras, and TensorFlow. 2nd ed. O'Reilly Media. 22. Chollet, F. (2018). Deep Learning with Python. Manning Publications.

**Chapter 12: Case Studies** 23. Davenport, T. H., & Ronanki, R. (2018). Artificial Intelligence for the Real World. Harvard Business Review. 24. McAfee, A., & Brynjolfsson, E. (2017). Machine, Platform, Crowd: Harnessing Our Digital Future. W.W. Norton & Company.

**Chapter 13: The Future of Work with AI** 25. West, D. M. (2018). The Future of Work: Robots, AI, and Automation. Brookings Institution Press. 26. Susskind, R., & Susskind, D. (2015). The Future of the Professions: How Technology Will Transform the Work of Human Experts. Oxford University Press.

**Chapter 14: AI Research and Development** 27. Russell, S. J., & Norvig, P. (2020). Artificial Intelligence: A Modern Approach. 4th ed. Pearson. 28. Schmidhuber, J. (2015). Deep Learning in Neural Networks: An Overview. Neural Networks, 61, 85-117.

**Chapter 15: Building an AI Strategy** 29. Bughin, J., Seong, J., Manyika, J., Chui, M., & Joshi, R. (2018). Notes from the AI Frontier: Insights from Hundreds of Use Cases. McKinsey Global Institute. 30. Agrawal, A., Gans, J. S., & Goldfarb, A. (2018). Prediction Machines: The Simple Economics of Artificial Intelligence. Harvard Business Review Press.

**Chapter 16: AI in Everyday Life** 31. Sundar Pichai. (2018). AI at Google: Our Principles. Google AI Blog. 32. Dwivedi, Y. K., et al. (2021). Artificial Intelligence (AI): Multidisciplinary Perspectives on Emerging Challenges, Opportunities, and Agenda for Research, Practice and Policy. International Journal of Information Management, 57, 101994.

**Chapter 17: AI and Cybersecurity** 33. Buczak, A. L., & Guven, E. (2016). A Survey of Data Mining and Machine Learning Methods for Cyber Security Intrusion Detection. IEEE Communications Surveys & Tutorials, 18(2), 1153-1176. 34. Sommer, R., & Paxson, V. (2010). Outside the Closed World: On Using Machine Learning for Network Intrusion Detection. 2010 IEEE Symposium on Security and Privacy.

**Chapter 18: Interdisciplinary Approaches to AI** 35. Kaplan, J., & Haenlein, M. (2019). Siri, Siri, in My Hand: Who's the Fairest in the Land? On the Interpretations, Illustrations, and Implications of Artificial Intelligence. Business Horizons, 62(1), 15-25. 36. Ertel, W. (2018). Introduction to Artificial Intelligence. 2nd ed. Springer.

**Chapter 19: Educational Resources for AI** 37. Chollet, F. (2017). Deep Learning with Python. Manning Publications. 38. Goodfellow, I., et al. (2016). Deep Learning. MIT Press.

**Chapter 20: Conclusion** 39. Tegmark, M. (2017). Life 3.0: Being Human in the Age of Artificial Intelligence. Knopf. 40. Harari, Y. N. (2018). 21 Lessons for the 21st Century. Spiegel & Grau.

# EPILOGUE

As we conclude our journey through the expansive and rapidly evolving world of Artificial Intelligence (AI), it's important to reflect on the transformative potential and the responsibilities that come with it. The advancements in AI over the past few years have been nothing short of remarkable, impacting various aspects of our lives, from the way we work to the way we interact with technology on a daily basis.

AI's role in revolutionizing industries such as healthcare, finance, retail, and manufacturing showcases its potential to drive significant efficiencies, enhance decision-making, and create new opportunities. Its interdisciplinary applications in art, creativity, and scientific research highlight AI's versatility and its capacity to push the boundaries of human ingenuity.

However, with great power comes great responsibility. The ethical considerations surrounding AI—such as privacy concerns, bias, fairness, and regulatory challenges—cannot be overlooked. It is crucial for developers, policymakers, and users to collaborate and establish frameworks that ensure the responsible and equitable deployment of AI technologies. Building ethical AI systems that are transparent, accountable, and fair is essential for gaining public trust and maximizing the benefits of AI.

Looking ahead, the future of AI is incredibly promising. Emerging trends like quantum computing, explainable AI, and federated learning are set to further enhance AI's capabilities and applications. The integration of AI with other cutting-edge technologies such as the Internet of Things (IoT) and blockchain will open up new frontiers and possibilities.

As you continue your exploration and engagement with AI, we encourage you to stay informed and proactive. The field of AI is dynamic and constantly evolving, making continuous learning and adaptation essential. Whether through formal education, online courses, industry conferences, or hands-on projects, keeping up with the latest developments will enable you to leverage AI effectively and responsibly.

We hope that "AI Revolution: Navigating the Future of Artificial Intelligence and Technology Trends" has provided you with valuable insights, practical knowledge, and a deeper understanding of the AI landscape. May this knowledge empower you to harness the potential of AI to innovate, solve complex problems, and contribute positively to society.

Thank you for embarking on this journey with us. The future of AI is bright, and together, we can navigate it towards a better and more inclusive world.

www.ingramcontent.com/pod-product-compliance
Lightning Source LLC
Chambersburg PA
CBHW071926210526
45479CB00002B/571